ALSO BY JAMES LORD

MYTHIC
GIACOMETTI

JAMES LORD

Farrar Straus Giroux | New York

MYTHIC
GIACOMETTI

Farrar, Straus and Giroux
19 Union Square West, New York 10003

Distributed in Canada by Douglas & McIntyre Ltd.
Printed in the United States of America
First edition, 2004

All translations are by the author.

Library of Congress Cataloging-in-Publication Data
Lord, James.
    Mythic Giacometti / James Lord.— 1st ed.
        p.   cm.
    ISBN 0-374-21880-3 (hc : alk. paper)
    1. Giacometti, Alberto, 1901–1966.   2. Sculptors—
France—Biography.   3. Giacometti, Alberto, 1901–
1966—Psychology.   I. Title.

NB553.G4L68 2004
730'.92—dc22
                                        2003060262

EAN: 978-0-374-21880-5

www.fsgbooks.com

1   3   5   7   9   10   8   6   4   2

Frontispiece: The Giacometti family in 1909: (*clockwise from left*)
Alberto, Bruno, Giovanni, Annetta, Ottilia, Diego

For Jonathan Galassi

FOREWORD

Alberto Giacometti was considered by his peers even during his lifetime to be a legendary figure, rousing, indeed, a certain awe by virtue of his selfless and indefatigable commitment to artistic creation. Since his death in 1966, his works have been widely and continually exhibited throughout the world, contributing for those who are by nature visionary a further perception of Giacometti's power to wrest from nothingness works which symbolize profound and enigmatic clues to the abstruse meaning of human experience. In this, as in much else, he knowingly stood alone in his century, the final embodiment of an artistic continuum comprising the redemptive grandeur of our entire civilization.

Such, in any case, is my conviction. Though hesitant to introduce myself personally into a quest for the deepest functions and implications of Alberto's life and accomplishment, no comparable undertaking has to my knowledge yet been carried out, and therefore I hesitantly take this step in my eightieth year. As I have stated elsewhere, Alberto and I were never close friends, but we were intimate acquaintances. Intimacy, to be sure, was the very definition of any relation, however casual, with Alberto. Accordingly, when the task of preparing his biography was proposed, I rashly agreed to try to put my best foot forward, so to speak, little surmising what endurance and discernment would be needed to follow in *his* footsteps. True, I was a writer and had written already several pieces about Alberto, especially a short book titled *A Giacometti Portrait*, in which I describe in detail what took place when in 1964 I posed before him for a painting. None of this occasional work, however, had provided me with the flimsiest notion of what a faithful biography of Alberto should strive to attain. The schooling in knowledge and judgment consequently became harsh and prolonged, lasting fifteen years.

I worked hard, fearfully mindful that only by surpassing my resources of imagination and intellect might I hope to stumble upon a vista of understanding. Luck was with me, as years forced understanding upon the uninvited visitor to terra incognita, where I thought to discern the silhouette of a structure which might contain an answer to the riddle of Alberto's existence. This surmise grew more forceful as the story of the artist's experience built, by itself, a basis more and more ineluctable upon which the structure and all its ramifications arose in a tragic revelation. The knowledge and architecture of this structure, which I cannot refrain from calling mythological, became the blueprint, as it were, for the edification of Alberto's biography. However, none of the designs or details of this "blueprint" were allowed to appear in my text, though I hinted at some of them, because it was neither the prerogative nor the business of the biographer to instruct the reader concerning what materials or expectations had presided over the edification — if I may challenge fate by naming it — of a monument. Yes, the biography became for its architect a monument dedicated to honor and perpetuate the memory, aspirations, and achievements of a legendary hero. Though no Ictinus, I did my painstaking best, and feel consequently that I owe it to Alberto to attempt to provide some finishing details of which the hero himself must mainly have been unaware. He could not, I believe, have lived with such awareness. But he had to live it out. This he did by working. In the end he may have come close to ultimate clairvoyance, but then, as always, he was prepared to pay the price. He had paid it, of course, as we all are born to do, from the very beginning. My farewell, then, to Alberto will be to try to elucidate the symbolic and mythological verities of his adventure in order further to embellish with his own truth a worthy monument to his heroism.

MYTHIC GIACOMETTI

1

Long before the ominous dawn of history, men were already creating myths in the hope of finding out who they were, where they had come from, and what fate awaited them in the inscrutable hereafter. What they sought many millennia ago, when time itself was measured by fire or ice, was little different from what we are looking for today: an explanation of the inexplicable. Mythic insight is concerned to elucidate the meaning of life. In order to do this one must follow the presumption of such meaning to its origin, to the idea of creation, of a Creator Himself, or Itself. A myth expresses in symbolic terms what is both metaphysical and ethical. No form of life, however, not even the human mind or spirit, is capable of illuminating once and for all the first cause of creation, which remains as mysterious to us as it was to prehistoric man. To be sure, we know more than he did. But is our understanding greater? What reason have we to assert that our myths are superior to his, since their purpose, now as then, is to define reality forever in absolute comprehension of the universe?

Life on earth arises from origins of suffering too

profound, tragic, and inexplicable to be adequately appreciated through a semblance of understanding or progress. The mystery of birth is inseparable from the mystery of death. This duality demands a symbolic interpretation, and accordingly the symbolism of mythology concerns the enigma of life in its totality. Myths, in short, be they of whatever spiritual origin, have evolved as patterns developed from the nucleus of all human relationships and, though they have yet to answer the prehistoric questions, are essential to the search for meaning in mankind's experiences.

Of all the heroes of Greek mythology, none is better known or has had greater impact upon the psychic constitution and social behavior of our planet's population than that of Oedipus, King of Thebes. His name and myth are nearly common knowledge today, popularized even by the cinema and famed for a century due to Freud's use of both in order to describe a psychological condition or complex theoretically characteristic of neurotic people. The myth of Oedipus was well known, of course, millennia before Freud, appearing in the *Iliad* and providing material for one of the enduring masterworks of world drama, *King Oedipus* by Sophocles, a fateful evocation of man's tragic search for identity. It has continued throughout subsequent centuries to compel the interest and admiration of discerning thinkers. Aristotle admired the myth and tragedy as perfect examples of tragic causality. Aeschylus, Euripides, and Seneca based dramas upon it. Freud affirmed that the primal sense of guilt amongst mankind as a whole, being the ultimate source of religion and morality, was acquired in the beginnings of history due to the Oedipus complex. Sexuality, after all, is the heartbeat of human life. Oedipus's doom is the outcome of his obdurate determination to confront truth, ineluctable and absolute.

The myth of Oedipus in its elementary form is widely known and, though difficult to understand, can be easily and briefly related. Laius, King of Thebes, and his wife, Jocasta, become parents to an infant son. Laius had been forewarned by the Delphic Oracle, however, that he was fated to be killed by his own son, who would then take Jocasta for his wife. It was decided, therefore, to do away with the infant. And although the father had personal reasons to fear the crime of infanticide, the mother was frightened by the prospect of incest; thus was the newborn child entrusted by Laius to a shepherd with orders to pierce one or both of his feet with a spike and leave him exposed on a mountainside to die. The baby was rescued, however, by another shepherd and brought to the childless rulers of Corinth, King Polybus and Queen Meropé, who gladly adopted the infant as their own, naming him, because of his cruel wound, Oedipus, which in Greek means "swollen foot." Honored as a prince of Corinth, Oedipus grew contentedly to manhood. Having occasion himself to consult the Delphic Oracle, he learned to his horror that his fate was to murder his father and marry his mother. Believing his foster parents to be his true father and mother, he fled Corinth in order to forestall such a fearful eventuality. At a lonely crossroads he encountered a traveler who irascibly ordered him out of the way, whereupon the young prince, ignorant of the man's identity, attacked him with his staff and killed him. This traveler, of course, was Laius, and thus was one half of the dread prophecy fulfilled. Continuing on his way toward Thebes, he found the city terrorized by the Sphinx, who, acting as a destructive agent of the gods, killed all who could not answer her riddle. In the absence of Laius, Jocasta's brother Creon, having assumed the role of regent, had vowed that the man who could rid the city of its fearsome scourge would be crowned king and take in marriage his sister, the widowed queen. Daring and audacious, Oedipus presented himself before the half-woman, half-beast and answered her riddle correctly, whereupon the Sphinx committed suicide. Received with homage and rejoicing in Thebes, where Creon kept his word, Oedipus was crowned and wed Jocasta. Thus, though unknowingly, he had carried out the oracle's dire prediction and embraced his doom. An era of enjoyment and uneventful prosperity nonetheless ensued, during which the incestuous royal couple begot two sons and two daughters. Then a dreadful pestilence was visited upon the city. Creon consulted the Delphic Oracle, who declared that the only way to rid the land of its pollution would be to learn the identity of Laius's assassin and expel him from Thebes. Oedipus determines, no matter what the consequences, to see that this is done. Through a series of increasingly painful and damning revelations, brilliantly dramatized by Sophocles, Oedipus courageously confronts the truth. The oracle has been horribly verified. The king himself is both assassin and incestuous spouse. Jocasta, overcome by consternation and despair, hangs herself; while Oedipus, in an agony of grief, puts out his eyes and departs forever from Thebes to wander in wretched remorse till death.

Now, it may seem untoward that a young fellow should kill an unknown wayfarer simply because he has been ordered, however rudely, to step aside at a lonely crossroads. But mythic symbolism is implacable. The order is given by the very man who is responsible for the fact that for Oedipus, a man with an injured foot, to take a step has a symbolic meaning which renders that order intolerable, rousing an otherwise illogical anger which is precisely the vengeance of a mutilated spirit, one which in symbolic terms is unable to stand upright. Nor is it any accident that the weapon of murder and retaliation happens to be the symbol of a fate ordained by Laius himself and of the oracle's sinister prediction: the staff, which the lame in antiquity bore as evidence of their infirmity. Meaningful also is the location of the crime, a crossroads, because it is there that Oedipus, having proven himself a man masterful enough to strike down anyone whose arrogance offended his most vulnerable singularity, determines to turn his steps toward a confrontation with the dreaded Sphinx, pleased to regard himself a conquering hero destined to achieve the highest degree of spiritual accomplishment, liberating the land from evil and distress and freeing himself from the fearful menace of the oracle.

The Sphinx's celebrated riddle, though existing in numerous versions, is fundamentally changeless, concerning the nature, the conduct, and the evolution of human life: "What manner of creature makes its way in the morning on four feet, at midday on two, and in the evening on three?" Oedipus, of all those challenged, was most apt to answer correctly, saying, "Man crawls on all fours as an infant, walks upright in the prime of life, and uses a staff in old age." It is profoundly meaningful that the riddle concerns the foot, symbol of the spirit and of life's perpetuation. In fact, the riddle is addressed to all mankind, because the true answer, for anyone, is "myself." And to solve the riddle is to be confronted by the fundamental philosophical challenge: "Know thyself." It is also significant that the riddle presents man as an animal, for mindless behavior reduces him to bestiality, and this, alas, Oedipus does not guess, failing to realize that the Sphinx's riddle alluded to his infirmity. Only perfect spiritual clairvoyance might have revealed that the riddle was the representation of his vital weakness, the inexpiable transgression still to come, of which he will be the hapless victim, despite a seeming mastery.

The Oedipus complex, drawn from the myth of Oedipus and advanced as axiomatic by Freud, designates attraction on the part of a child toward the parent of the opposite sex and rivalry and hostility toward the parent of its own. This occurs approximately during the years three to five, resolution presumed normally to occur thereafter by identification with the parent of the same sex and by renunciation of sexual interest in the parent of the opposite sex. Freud considered this complex to be the nucleus of all human relationships. While acknowledging the significance of Oedipal influences upon personality development, many contemporary psychiatrists consider resentment of parental authority more influential than sexual rivalry.

Mythic purpose does not wait upon the best intentions of those fated to serve it. Giovanni Giacometti and his wife, Annetta, decided by common consent to name their firstborn child, a son, Giovanni Alberto Giacometti. The deliberate sameness of name between father and son can hardly have led the parents to crave or anticipate a sameness of enterprise or aspiration. In all innocence, of course, that was nevertheless their first mistake, a grave one for a beginning, if mythic destiny can, in fact, be construed to have a discernible beginning. As it would have been excessive, to say the least, to have two Giovannis in one household, the child was always called Alberto, and that name certainly suited him, for it means "illustrious through nobility." What the son may have felt or thought about bearing the same name as his father must remain forever a matter of conjecture, because he never mentioned the fact, never signed a work from his hand with that name, never saw it printed in an exhibition catalogue or newspaper interview. Perhaps he more or less forgot that the name he made world famous did not divulge an entire truth. To be sure, it must have appeared on his passport, but that document was seen only by officials who knew nothing about the meaning to an artist of his name. Very few people outside the immediate family, I suspect, were aware that Alberto was also Giovanni, and I myself learned of it only when research led me to acquire a copy of Alberto's marriage certificate. That a vital truth about his birth should have come to light by virtue of his marriage is meaningful to an extent which can hardly be exaggerated and of which the light, indeed, may seem almost blinding when it comes time to consider that extraordinary event.

Few people are chosen, pursued, seized, liberated, and celebrated by destiny. And that is doubtless just as well, for a destiny is a lifelong business. It will never let one go, nor will it ever let one down, whatever glory or infamy may lie in store. It demands to be followed from beginning to end along a road never traveled by anyone else, and its terminus—its destination—is not only the grave but the attainment of enduring legend, the mythic stature which mankind loves to idolize in order to mitigate the consternation of enigmatic life in an incomprehensible universe.

The myth of Oedipus and the complex named for it are fundamental constituents of the life and art of Alberto Giacometti. His destiny, to be sure, did not duplicate the classic, Sophoclean scenario in a specific, chronological manner, and it would be foolhardy to contend that Alberto was, so to speak, a contemporary Oedipus. And yet . . . and yet the likenesses and coincidences (if any fateful similarity can be considered truly to lack causal relation) are such that impartial judgment must suggest that this artist's destiny was Oedipal to an extent so significant that it became part and parcel of his heroic adventure. This, of course, is a challenge to discernment. The prospect of verifiable understanding is elusive, but it may lead to persuasive revelations if pursued with perseverance. The materials of the mythic structure of any individual's existence are rarely, if ever, set in place in such an orderly, foreordained manner as for Oedipus, King of Thebes, who was himself, after all, a purposeful creation of mythology. They are more likely to be assembled at random rather than added bit by logical bit to the coherent edifice of a destiny. An element essential to the foundation may not be provided until the structure itself is half-finished, and vice versa. This was certainly the case for Alberto. What is telling and indispensable is that the revelatory element ultimately finds a place, the one and only place, where it can foreshadow the mystery of a human life.

Alberto was but six months old when his mother once more became pregnant, which caused her to wean her firstborn. Weaning at six or seven months is not unusual. At any age, however, it may bring a loss of that sense of primal security, of physical certainty and delight, which every infant experiences through contact with his mother's body. On the fifteenth of November 1902, a second son was born to Annetta and Giovanni Giacometti. He was named Diego, after Velázquez, whom his father admired, and he was to dedicate himself with selfless devotion to the work and well-being of his older brother for nearly forty years of his own life.

While Alberto was still a very small child—barely more than an infant, though after the birth of Diego—he was frequently to be found in his father's studio.

For the mother it was easier to look after one child at a time, and Giovanni as he worked could, without inconvenience, keep half an eye on his older son. Thus, coalescent with the primal development of his awareness of the world in which he must make a place for himself, Alberto became familiar with the surroundings and materials of a professional artist, and in this context he performed the very first artistic act of which memory has retained the circumstances. It was, however, a destructive rather than a creative act, because what Alberto did was to discolor one of his father's paintings. The true fact of the matter, though, is that he smeared upon it a very particular color, for as often occurs in the case of an infant, his own excrement provided him with material for his amusement, assuming that that is what it was, and accordingly added a vital and very messy symbolism to the fate of the father's creation. The destructive act brought about no punitive consequences, of course, since no intent could reasonably be presumed. Family consensus naturally regarded the infantile act as such, but it was nonetheless never completely consigned to forgetfulness. When mentioned, however, it was recalled with the humorous and right-thinking assumption that childish is as childish does, nothing more. Small children may not have conscious knowledge of the motives which determine their acts; but that knowledge exists, survives, and possesses, so to speak, knowledge of itself. Such knowledge can be dangerous. An artist's creation is a manifestation of faith in the prerogative of his birthright, a symbol of his will to represent himself as supreme in a world of his making and above all an affirmation of man's obsessive craving for immortality. To deface or destroy an artist's creation is an act of aggression meant to deny the legitimacy of his raison d'être, to belittle the extent of his accomplishment, and to affirm that death for him will be definitive and in every respect evidence of nothingness. A profoundly meaningful adumbration of Alberto's mythic destiny had come about with fateful earliness.

The very first memory which in later life Alberto asserted that he retained of his childhood was an image of his mother. Writing of it later, he said, "The long black dress which touched the ground troubled me by its mystery; it seemed to be a part of the body, and that caused a feeling of fear and confusion." The child must have been two or three years old, at least, when he formed this image. His mother was thirty-two. Alberto's reaction is surprising and attracts attention. Confusion and fear are not feelings which most people associate with childhood memories of their mothers. To be sure, powerful psychic forces from later periods often shape and color the memories that seem to remain from childhood, and though children's memories do retain what is important, a kind of symbolic representation often occurs which is not unlike the symbolism of fantasies or dreams. That Alberto was troubled by the mystery of his mother's dress which seemed part of her body, causing fear and confusion, should not be surprising, because the mystery concerns the sexual interest of every child, which is directed primarily to the problem of birth, leading him to wonder what sort of intimacy exists between his parents. He wants to see what goes on when they are alone, and this impulse to see, the importance of it, the ability, the act of looking or watching, and all the circumstances of vision, are intensified by the longing to know what is at the basis of life. A certain dread, however, is inevitably provoked by his inability to pierce this mystery by grasping the facts of sexuality, which lie concealed behind the mother's clothing. Both the longing and the fear coalesce in the childish unconscious, rousing a desire for greater intimacy with the mother than would be possible, or tolerable. However, it exists, this desire—it may be lifelong—and its power seeks expression by symbolic means.

When Alberto had lately passed his fourth birthday, the family moved to a neighboring village in the mountainous valley, Stampa, and there they remained for three quarters of a century in modest but comfortable lodgings. The move was a happy one for Alberto, because he had reached the age when his curiosities and desires relating to nature could more happily and easily be explored than around Borgonovo. A tumultuous mountain stream coursed through the center of Stampa, and beyond it steep meadows studded with glacial boulders rose to the peak of the valley's highest mountain, the Piz Duan. Concealed beneath one of these boulders lay a cave caused by erosion. Alberto's father took him to visit it for the first time not long after the family's arrival. One cannot help musing upon the significance of the paternal initiative inasmuch as the importance of the cave became momentous for the son. The entrance was a long, low slit between stone and earth like a half-open mouth or, given an imaginative predilection, some other giant orifice of human likeness. The interior was dim and low, narrowing at the rear to a rounded space nearly hidden and dark. Though the cave was known to all the children of Stampa, Alberto had an exclusive feeling for it not shared by his brother or other playmates. "From the first," he later wrote, "I considered that stone a friend, a being full of good intentions toward me . . . like someone one has known long before and loved, then found again with surprise and infinite joy." Every morning when he awoke, his first concern was to look out the window to make sure that the stone was still there, and even from a distance he felt able to distinguish its minutest details. Nothing else in the landscape interested him. For several years the cave was the most important place on earth—or, one should say, in the earth. His greatest pleasure, he said, came when he penetrated as deeply as possible into the narrow crevice at the rear of the cave. "I attained the height of joy," he asserted. "All my desires were fulfilled." The fulfillment, to be sure, was symbolic, but the desires were not. They are felt by all children, though Alberto's case was exceptional. It called for expression. One day, the little boy thought that he might need some nourishment while curled up securely in the depths of the cave. So he took from his mother's kitchen a portion of bread, carried it to the cave, and hid it deep in the recess at the rear. Once he had done that, his satisfaction must have seemed to be the greatest that life can give, for in a sense he never got over it. The passionate attachment to the cave, and especially to its depths, was clearly a nostalgia for the womb and a desire to be physically united with Mother Earth. The portion of bread from his mother's kitchen—the proverbial "staff of life"—brought her symbolically into Alberto's hidden life, sustaining it and him not only by her presence but also by her unknowing confirmation of a secret experience.

One day, while playing near the cave, Alberto wandered a bit farther afield than usual. "I would not be able to remember by what chance," he later wrote. It's odd that he felt compelled to preface his account with a failure of memory and the intervention of chance. In truth he recalled only too well what happened, and chance had nothing to do with the consequences.

> I found myself on a rise in the ground. In front of me, a little below in the midst of brush, rose up an enormous black stone in the form of a narrow, pointed pyramid, of which the sides were almost vertical. I cannot express the emotion of resentment and confusion I experienced at that moment. The stone struck me at once as a living being, hostile, threatening. It threatened everything: us, our games, our cave. Its existence was unbearable to me and I felt immediately—being unable to make it disappear—that I must take no notice of it, forget it, and speak of it to no one. Nevertheless, I did go close to it, but with a feeling of surrendering to something reprehensible, secret, improper. I barely touched it with one hand in disgust and fear. Trembling at the pros-

pect of finding an entrance, I walked around it. No sign of a cave, which made the stone even more unbearable to me, and yet I did experience one satisfaction: an opening in that stone would have complicated everything and I already felt the desolation of our cave if it had become necessary to be concerned with another at the same time. I ran away from the black stone, I didn't mention it to the other children, I dismissed it and never went back to see it again.

That Alberto should have remembered this incident with such detailed clarity many years later, should have felt impelled to describe it in writing and to make public and permanent such a strange, intimate aspect of his childhood by publishing the account in a literary review, is more than reason enough, if any at all were needed, to search for the symbolic meaning of his experience. The black, erect, pointed, living, hostile, unbearable stone seemed in all likelihood to have been a representation for this child of that part of the male anatomy most secret, hidden, menacing, portentous, and aggressive, albeit at the same time a source of pleasure condemned by conventional morality and the awesome, mysterious, fortuitous donor of life. Namely, the paternal penis. To a child who sought and found bliss in the entrails of Mother Earth, where he enjoyed indispensable nourishment taken from her, the stone's symbolic presence could only have roused unbearable confusion and resentment, because it threatened the fulfillment of the self hidden in his cave. | 17

And yet, with a sense of surrender to what is reprehensible and secret, he nevertheless approached the stone and touched it with disgust and fear. The games of children are rightly regarded by adults as child's play, because a child cannot be judged by a moral and legal code as if mature and lucid. Alberto probably did not speak to his parents of his encounter with the black stone, but it did occur, and such experiences in childhood have vital significance both as evidence of innate constitutional tendencies and inasmuch as they cause and foster later development. They provide insight into the child's sexual life, and so into that of humanity as a whole. The symbolic meaning of Alberto's encounter with the black stone—and his devotion to the cave—would more forcefully than ever demonstrate the oracular power and strategic instrumentality of the mythic affirmation in his life. Nor is it idle to speculate already that the encounter with the black stone would reverberate, so to speak, in the first of the two most dramatic and traumatic adult events of his lifetime.

During these early years, Alberto formed an obsessive habit which seemed odd, though innocent, to the other members of his family. Every night before going to sleep, he took particular care in the arrangement of his shoes and socks on the floor beside the bed. The socks were flattened and laid out side by side so that each had the appearance of a foot in silhouette, the shoes placed in a precise position beside them. This painstaking ritual, repeated without variation every night, amused Alberto's brothers, and sometimes, to tease him, they would disrupt his arrangement, provoking outbursts of rage. For the rest of his life, Alberto continued to be obsessively concerned with this arrangement of socks and shoes before going to sleep. His passion did not extend to other articles of clothing, however; only the socks and shoes. It belabors the obvious to interpret this obsession as the intimation to an immature mind of the symbolic significance of the foot, both spiritual and sexual, the foot as the guiding symbolic factor in pursuing life's unpredictable and perplexing path, the foot also as a source of gratification in acts of deviant perversity. The safety and protection of the foot, both physically and symbolically, is naturally of vital concern to one marked for a mythic destiny. Mention of Oedipus in this context is superfluous but compelling. Alberto would have to wait some thirty years till fate took pains to endow him with the telltale infirmity of the Theban king, and that was the second of the two dramatic events he himself affirmed to have been decisive for his art and life.

Giovanni Giacometti occasionally made short trips to Geneva, Paris, and elsewhere to visit friends or endeavor to further the slow progress of his career. During one of these periodic absences, Alberto suddenly found himself unable to recall his father's physical appearance. This failure of memory, seemingly equivalent to a deliberate elimination of the paternal presence, is especially surprising inasmuch as the house in Stampa contained numerous self-portraits, portraits, and photographs of Giovanni. Distraught by his incomprehensible amnesia, Alberto burst into tears and began screaming, "I can't remember my father's face." His brother Diego, to whom he turned for consolation, simply laughed and said, "You know, he's that little man with the red beard." The temporary amnesia may have been incomprehensible to Alberto, but it looms with meaning upon dispassionate and forewarned consideration. Though the fatal crossroads still lay distant, it could not now be passed by with impunity en route toward the confrontation of Alberto Giacometti with himself.

On the fifth of August 1911, Annetta Giacometti reached the age of forty. To celebrate that event, she made an outing to the border town of Castasegna with her husband and four children—a daughter, Ottilia, and a third son, Bruno, having been born in 1904 and 1907, respectively. While in Castasegna, they posed for a local photographer. His picture is a remarkable document. Diego, seated in the foreground, looks ill at ease, his hair cut short, while the luxuriant locks of his older brother are still long. Ottilia, wistful and pensive, kneels between father and mother. Giovanni is seated in the center of the group, but he does not dominate it; holding his youngest son on his right knee, he glances downward, an expression of contentment on his gentle features. Bruno appears placid, almost impassive. Annetta, attired in her long black dress with a flowered shirtwaist, is seated to the extreme right and is the largest figure in the group. She sits calmly, her hands joined, looking at Alberto, who is opposite her on the far side of the group, and he returns her look with a stare of rapt fixity. It is the intensity, the quality, and the meaning of

their reciprocal gaze which dominates the picture. Of

lighted, for Alberto received enthusiastic, affectionate encouragement. He had not yet to fight to accomplish what satisfaction he sought.

In the autumn of 1915, Alberto entered a boarding school at Schiers, a small village about fifty miles due north of Stampa. By that time he had already turned his hand to sculpture, enlisting the ever-compliant Diego as model, and the result showed an instinctive grasp of artistic form, surpassing sensitivity, and exceptional technical virtuosity. A couple of years later, Alberto for the first time modeled a bust of his mother. It is strikingly unlike the one he had previously made of Diego. The act of the artist had formerly been subordinate to the presence of the model. No longer. It is the artist, now, and he alone, who imparts life to the work of art. That the work in which Giacometti first seems to have asserted his dominance as a creative individual should have been a portrait of his mother should not surprise us. Just as the artist has come nearer to us, however, the model is placed at a distance, as if Alberto had been unprepared or unable to approach her any more closely than he allows us to. He has determined not only how we shall see the individual but also our relation to her in space. The early bust of Diego shows the child present at the very surface of the sculpture, but Annetta Giacometti in person is situated beyond the bronze integument of her effigy, and the ambiguous expression which Alberto has given to her eyes seems to imply that there may never be a way for anyone to cross that frontier. The bent for portraiture, however, was not directed toward his father for another decade or more, when he

this the others are unaware, as if Annetta and her eldest son were in fact alone together. Everything about
Alberto, his clothes, his posture, even his physical existence, seems subordinate to the spellbound gaze
which he fixes upon his mother, her person combin-
ing absolute fascination with incommensurable mystery. She returns her son's gaze with regal equanimity,
appearing utterly sure of herself and of him. Whatever his gaze may portend, she looks serenely satisfied
with it, and with the world. Upon her lips there is an
enigmatic smile. Had she ever guessed, though, what
his gaze did mythically portend, her seeming serenity
would surely have reflected dismay, her smile an expression of foreboding.

Aged thirteen or fourteen, Alberto began to draw
consistently from nature. "I had the feeling," he said,
"that I had such a command over what I wanted to do
that I could do it exactly."

I admired myself, I felt that with such a formida-
ble means as drawing I could accomplish anything, that I could draw anything, that I saw more
clearly than anyone else. I drew in order to com-
municate and to dominate. I had the feeling of
being able to reproduce and possess whatever I
wanted. I became overbearing. Nothing could resist me. My pencil was my weapon.

The Giacometti family must have been surprised by
this sudden outburst of precocity—especially the father, who had more reason than the rest to view it
with interest. But everyone seems to have been de-

had already spent five years in Paris and was on the way to achieving his first success there.

If, however, the youthful artist had no inclination for the time being to exercise his powers by making a portrait of his artist father, he still did not balk at taking willful liberties with a portrait executed by someone else. In the family apartment at Stampa stood a small plaster bust of Giovanni, a likeness created long before, by a Swiss colleague called Rodo, a friend, deceased in 1913 in Munich, hence the bust was a souvenir of bygone camaraderie and aspirations shared. This work of art did not appeal to the subject's eldest son. He found it disagreeable, unlike his own image of his father, and so he decided to remake it in that image. Taking palette and brush, one day while his father was briefly absent, he completely painted the white plaster. "I was satisfied with the result," he later asserted. "I found that only then was the bust finished, only then was it a portrait of my father—and I was sure I had done the most important work on it. My father was a little surprised. Maybe he thought I hadn't shown enough respect for Rodo's work, but he didn't reproach me for it." This was further evidence, indeed, of Giovanni's unusually tolerant and gentle nature. Unusual tolerance, though, can upon occasion be an easy way to fight shy of acts that are intolerably unusual.

While still at Schiers, Alberto contracted the mumps. Well past the age of puberty, he was not properly cared for, with the result that he also suffered an acute attack of orchitis, an inflammation and swelling of the testicles, causing intense physical pain and an emotional discomfort probably even more difficult to bear. The swollen testicles must have seemed to present both physically and psychically a serious threat to manhood, and they did. Acute attacks of orchitis last for several days and may have a grave aftereffect, for they frequently leave the patient sterile for life. That is what happened to Alberto. Accordingly, while hardly more than a boy, one of life's most basic and far-reaching decisions was made for him by nature, as it were, rather than by himself. An important turning point—a metaphorical crossroads—in every individual's existence is reached when sexual experience is subordinated to the purposes of reproduction, and it is a characteristic common to all sexual abnormalities that, in them, reproduction as an aim has been set aside. That decisive turning point was peremptorily eliminated from Alberto's future before he had had an opportunity to experience any normal sexual life whatever. He was condemned to a lifetime of equivocal activity in the most intimate realm of human experience, because the pursuit of physical gratification for its own sake was all that his sexual capacity allowed. Since he could never be a father, he could never be fully a husband, and so he was deprived forever not only of a normal sexual life but also of a normal social life. It would have been surprising had this not caused some demoralization as regards fulfillment of the masculine role. A feeling of genital insecurity and the awareness of sterility can contribute very powerfully toward problems of impotence.

Thus, a fateful psychic wound had been suffered by the young artist at the outset of his maturity. Given his masterful temperament, however, he made the best of this, and, indeed, one may reasonably remark that he made the most of it. His entire experience as a human being, after all, was purposefully placed at the service of his aspiration. If wounds and combats and even challenging mysteries were to be encountered en route, then they, too, would have to serve, and he was prepared to expend whatever part of life's constitutive principle might be necessary in order to overcome all threats save one. He had been prepared, of course, from the beginning.

Having put Schiers permanently behind him, it became clear that Alberto was to become, following in his father's footsteps, an artist. Giovanni asked whether he thought to be a painter or sculptor. Alberto said, "Both." The parents agreed. Annetta's motives and emotions may have been more complex than those of her husband, but the sincerity of her agreement was certainly wholehearted. "After all," Alberto later observed, "she had married a painter." The promising young artist was sent to study at the School of Fine Arts in Geneva, a city which he immediately disliked. Supported by his parents, he persevered. This important material relation between Alberto and his family, which prolonged the physical dependence of childhood, was to last many years longer.

If the eighteen-year-old artist disliked Geneva, he also disliked the traditional teaching at his school. The recollection of two intriguing incidents from those long-ago times have nonetheless survived. One day in the drawing class a buxom model named Loulou was posing nude. Convention required that | 25 students draw the entire figure, but Alberto maintained that it was his prerogative to draw only what interested him. To the great irritation of the instructor, he stubbornly and repeatedly drew enormous studies of the girl's foot. On another occasion during a class for sculpture in stone an incident occurred which made such an impression on the friend working beside Alberto that fifty years later it remained his most vivid memory of the young Giacometti. In the midst of his work, Alberto inadvertently knocked from his sculpture stand the heavy steel hammer he had been using. It fell from a height of almost a meter directly onto his foot. A normal reaction would have been to "displace" the pain by some physical compensation, to cry out or jump up and down. But Alberto remained absolutely motionless and made no sound whatsoever. A grimace of pain twisted his features, then he bent down, picked up the hammer, and went on working as if nothing had happened. That the symbolism of the foot was decisive needed no confirmation, but it added to itself as the years added to its meaning.

In the spring of 1920 Giovanni was appointed a member of the committee sent to Venice by the Swiss government to inspect the national pavilion at the great biannual exhibition of art, the famed Biennale, then still the most prestigious artistic event in the Western world. He took his eldest son with him. This first visit to the fabulous city of love and death was a thrilling revelation to Alberto, who was especially excited by the many paintings of Tintoretto. During the early autumn of that same year he returned for a time to the art school in Geneva, but the experience of the previous spring had aroused feelings and desires which made that inhibited and inhibiting city seem tedious. He longed to return to Italy, and to Venice. As usual, he was allowed to do as he pleased.

Arriving in Florence in mid-November, he found the city freezing cold. Uncomfortable and lonely, he decided after a month to move on to Rome, where he would be welcomed in the home of familiar cousins. The Roman Giacomettis were impressed by the articulate verve and artistic skills of their country cousin but slightly embarrassed by his unrefined manners and the shabby clothes handed down from his father. Quickly aware that he seemed gauche amidst the grandeur of the ancient and modern capital, Alberto promptly set things right by acquiring a fashionable new suit, fine overcoat, scarf, and gloves, even a walking stick which pleased him most in his emergence as a young man of fashion. Since canes were no longer the staple of masculine elegance which they had been twenty years before—too many crippled veterans could not get along without one—it may have seemed a bit eccentric for Alberto in the bloom of health to carry one. If so, that didn't trouble him, and he flourished it with a swagger.

Bianca, the eldest of Alberto's six young Roman cousins, lively, saucy, pretty, was fifteen when her nineteen-year-old relative from Stampa came to visit. She alone in the Giacometti family didn't much care for Alberto, and he quickly fell in love with her. It was the first overt, unhappy love of his adult life. He persuaded her to pose for a bust, but she disliked both posing and the bust, which she petulantly destroyed when the artist's professional and personal persistence became too pressing. Needless to say, there was no physical intimacy between Alberto and Bianca. He felt trepidation at the prospect of sexual experience because it was related to notions of love and personal commitment. Probably the painful attack of orchitis, and its consequences, had left him with a sense of genital inadequacy, and also of sexual apprehension. But there was something more, some interdiction that made the sexual act seem not only intimidating but frightening. Desire, however, overcame apprehension, because the sole fulfillment of sexuality is sexual experience.

Having rented a small studio in which to work, Alberto persuaded a prostitute to accompany him there to draw her. Then he slept with her. He literally exploded with enthusiasm, he said. "It's cold!" he shouted. "It's mechanical!" This explosion, charged with the energy and release of a youthful orgasm, altered forever the configuration of Alberto's inner self. The sexual act was mechanical. It was cold. Therefore, it need have, it could have, nothing to do with love. It was not to be feared. It entailed no commitment of one's identity. No dire consequences could stem from it. A thrilling sense of freedom appears to have followed the cataclysm, and the enthusiasm with which Alberto greeted it can only be construed as a measure of his previous foreboding. He cannot, however, have imagined that the passion with which he embraced his liberation was in direct proportion to the dispassion with which he embraced his liberator.

His first mature sexual experience established a pattern. Prostitutes became overnight the simplest solution to an insoluble problem. It was not yet necessary to justify this expedience. Physical deliverance did that. But the time would come when he felt constrained to explain, repeatedly, in public and private, why whores made the most satisfactory mistresses. It was courageous of him to do that, because, while the reasons he gave were serious and sincere, none of them hinted at the true reason. It lay too close to his heart. But he was in no danger of being obliged to understand, for his work fulfilled the function of understanding.

While in Italy, the young artist was anxious to visit Naples, Pompeii, and the Greek temples at Paestum. Traveling with a young English acquaintance, Alberto went south from Rome on March 31, 1921. He was delighted with Naples, its museums, palaces, and the splendid bay. After three days the young travelers took the train to Paestum, about sixty miles due south and close by the sea. In 1921 that magical site had not yet become a noisy attraction of industrial tourism. The three Doric temples, as fine and well preserved as any surviving, stood in serene solitude among pines and oleanders. Alberto was deeply moved by this peaceful and forgotten precinct, especially by the great, nearly intact temple to Poseidon, that powerful and vengeful deity, worshiped not only as a ruler of the seas but also as a god of fertility. The relation of man to the immensity of the temple particularly impressed him and he said that he felt more religious spirit there than in all the Christian churches of Italy, adding that Paestum would remain forever in his memory. It would, indeed, and one may actually wonder whether in his unconscious mind the supernatural importance of that particularly Greek sanctuary may not have been latent long before he ever set foot there. Having spent one night nearby, the two young men took the morning train to Pompeii. Alberto was reminded of his father, who had long ago spent a difficult, impoverished period of his life in a neighboring village before becoming one of Switzerland's most eminent painters. As it happened, that morning they were not alone in the railway carriage and presently a fellow passenger engaged them in conversation. He was a foreign gentleman, elderly and white-haired, speaking Italian with a guttural accent, a voyager traveling alone, pleased by an opportunity to chat with two high-spirited youths. And it is true that Alberto possessed exceptional charm, good humor, and eloquence. However, the encounter was brief, because the young men got off at Pompeii, while their casual acquaintance went on to Naples. As Alberto prepared to visit the city buried alive by Vesuvius, it was doubtless unknown to him that in the symbolism of dreams, travel by train is thought to represent a premonition of death. He was thrilled by the well-preserved place resurrected from its doom.

Now, at this time Bianca was enrolled at a boarding school in Switzerland, near Zurich. So that she would not have to travel so far by herself, it was arranged that Alberto should accompany her to Maloja, where his parents were established for the summer, and after
spending a night there she could take the train from

nearby Saint-Moritz. They set out together early in July. There was some delay en route. When they reached the frontier, it was closed till the next morning and they were obliged to go to a hotel for the night. After dining with her cousin, Bianca went to her room, undressed, and in her shift sat down to write a letter to her mother. Presently Alberto knocked on the door. Bianca, reluctant to open, demanded to know what he wanted. "I want to draw your feet," said Alberto. Thinking the request ridiculous, the young girl did not hesitate to say so, but her cousin knew how to insist and persuade. Finally she felt it would be easier to acquiesce than to resist, though she protested all the while that the business was absurd. But Alberto was in earnest. He came in with his paper and pencil and made drawings of Bianca's feet till midnight, when he contentedly returned to his own room. He had every reason to be satisfied, for sexual impulses which plainly appear as displaced and neurotic have contributed invaluable resources to the highest artistic, cultural, and social achievements of the human mind. Alberto and his cousin parted the following day and did not meet again for some years, yet the two would always remain in affectionate contact with each other.

A strange advertisement appeared in a Roman newspaper in the midsummer of 1921. The strangeness, indeed, is tantalizing, to say the least, because the advertisement certainly appeared and had dramatic consequences, but years of diligent research have been unable to resurrect it from the morgues of the Italian press, decimated by vandalism and flood. It had been inserted by a Dutchman from The Hague and was addressed to the attention of an anonymous young Swiss-Italian art student whom he had met some months before while traveling by train from Paestum to Naples. The latter was requested to respond by mail. Every law of probability would have seemed to be defied by the likelihood that this advertisement might ever be seen by the young man for whom it was intended. Mere probability, however, becomes irrelevant when the law of mythic determinism is prescribed. Antonio Giacometti, Bianca's father, chanced to notice the advertisement, chanced to suppose that it might conceivably be addressed to his young cousin, and therefore snipped it from the newspaper and took the trouble to send it on to Switzerland. Alberto was surprised and puzzled. He did recall having encountered an elderly foreigner in a railway compartment the previous April but could not imagine why this person should take so much trouble to reestablish contact with him four months later. Perhaps, he thought, the man had lost something precious en route and hoped that a fellow traveler might help him to recover it. Since the advertisement had miraculously reached its destination, Alberto, ever kind-hearted and conscientious, wrote to The Hague. An astonishing reply presently came back from a man named Peter van Meurs. He explained that although their previous meeting had indeed been brief, he had found the young artist an exceptionally agreeable traveling companion and proposed to renew the acquaintance. Enjoying travel, he explained, but being elderly and alone in the world, he preferred not to travel by himself. Therefore it would give him great pleasure if Alberto should agree to accompany him in Italy on a trip for which he would gladly defray all expenses. It was, to say the least, an unconventional proposition. It would have seemed still less conventional if the recipient had known more about his would-be benefactor.

Peter Antoni Nicolaus Stephanus van Meurs was born of Protestant parents at Arnhem in 1860, the first of six children. He studied law and obtained a degree but never practiced. He preferred to accept tedious but politic and respectable employment with the Central State Archives in The Hague, and in 1913 he was appointed Keeper of Public Records. In addition to professional duties, he assumed certain civic responsibilities, of which the most significant was as member of the board of directors of an organization formed to deal more humanely with delinquent young boys. He also belonged to the Society for the Furtherance of Sunday Rest and was an enthusiastic member of the Dutch Alpine Society. His love of travel therefore took him frequently to the mountains of northern Italy. He was a vegetarian, independently wealthy, and unmarried. This was the man who after an hour's accidental meeting aboard a train had gone to extraordinary lengths to renew contact with Alberto and now proposed to take him on a journey. To observe that the nineteen-year-old youth had made a potent impression on his fellow traveler of sixty-one is a surpassing understatement. The prospect of taking a trip in Italy appealed to Alberto, but he didn't know quite what to think of van Meurs's offer and turned to his brother for advice. There was no doubt in Diego's mind. He felt sure that the older man was a homosexual who planned to take advantage of the trip in order to enjoy an intimate adventure far from home with a foreign and unfamiliar youth unlikely to endanger his reputation. What other explanation, he argued, could there possibly be for the extravagant pains taken by this elderly stranger to reestablish contact and propose travel with a youth he had known but for an hour four months before? If his intentions had been innocent, why would he not have sought at home a traveling companion who spoke his language, whose companionship he knew to be agreeable and character trustworthy? And why, as a matter of fact, had he selected Alberto, an Italian-speaking lad, as a prospective companion rather than the young Englishman who had also been present? Would the English boy have been, perhaps, a little too close to home? By nature contradictory, not to say contrary, Alberto insisted that Diego's very reasonable observations were unfair and discreditable and he declined to take account of them. The fact was, however, that he had already made similar assumptions himself but despite misgivings did not choose to acknowledge them. He wrote to van Meurs and accepted. In later years he explained away this paradoxical acceptance by saying that he had been anxious to travel but was too poor to do so on his own. The explanation is almost as poignant as the proposition.

While working on Alberto's biography, when I came to the intervention of van Meurs, I wrote that
he was probably but not certainly homosexual and

that, lacking any evidence to the contrary, it seemed fair to assume that his intentions were innocent. To be sure, when speaking of the incident and its consequences, of which he spoke repeatedly, and indeed, mentioned in writing, Alberto never intimated that anything untoward or unwelcome had taken place between the older man and himself. He was expert, however, at rearranging facts to fit a more significant reality. As a biographer I felt that it was not my prerogative to make unwarranted assumptions for the reader. Today I feel differently, and the narrative I am composing now is not a biography but an exegesis with biographical implications. Diego's comments were superlatively sensible and shrewdly convincing. The evidence leading to a conclusion that van Meurs was not only homosexual but harbored improper expectations in extending his invitation is admittedly circumstantial, but any other explanation of his purpose would have to suggest a resolve quixotic to the frontier of folly, and this is decidedly not conduct in accord with the respectable trust of a Keeper of the Public Records. Moreover, one must wonder what desire had in the first place brought a man enamored of mountains to a region where there were none save ash-encrusted Vesuvius, not an alluring slope for a dedicated climber. And indeed one may wonder whether a man conscientiously committed to the humane treatment of delinquent young boys had journeyed to this part of the peninsula in order to gratify so worthy a purpose. It is a notorious fact that in the early decades of the last century many men sexually attracted by boys traveled south across the Alps from staid northern climes in search of the economical consummation of their desires popularly and willingly provided by handsome Italian youths. Being homosexual myself, and having traveled through southern Italy half a century ago, I know this to have been commonly the case. Good sense therefore argues against the innocence of Mr. van Meurs, and the argument seems conclusive when one judiciously considers the lifelong aftereffects for Alberto of the Dutchman's brief appearance. It is not my intent to censure the likely intentions of a man who, like myself, must have been made miserable by a burdensome secret, nor do I mean to judge the anomaly of Alberto's reaction to events more dramatic than even he supposed. I wish only to plead for the right of very peculiar circumstances to speak clearly—to cry out, indeed—for themselves. If this be presumption, destiny *did* make the most of it.

Van Meurs was evidently in a hurry to take advantage of his good luck, because it was agreed that the trip should begin soon, its itinerary leading the two travelers in early September across the Tyrolean Alps to Venice, the city Alberto had longed to revisit since leaving it a year before with his father. What Alberto's family thought of his plans we do not know, but they must have felt that he was old enough to make decisions for himself, because they saw to it that he did not depart penniless and accompanied him to his place of departure to wish him Godspeed.

Where and when in northern Italy the two met is unclear. Wherever the meeting occurred, it must have been a strange moment, tense with curiosity and ambiguity, as the two came face to face: an impetuous, creative youth of nineteen and a fanciful, graying gentleman of sixty-one. Van Meurs had thick, fleshy features and pronounced pouches under small eyes, but his chin was strong and his mouth firm. His shoulders were rather stooped, no doubt the result of decades spent poring over archives. Still, he looked like a man of purposeful resolve. The travelers set out through the Valtellina, a fertile agricultural valley, in 1921 still a backward region, where no motorized transport yet existed, and it was necessary to travel by the horse-drawn post coach over narrow, twisting roads up the faces of cliffs and above precipitous gorges. Their destination that day, September 3, was a small village high in the mountains called Madonna di Campiglio. Even in early September, it can grow quite cold at five thousand feet. When they reached the little place in a fold of the mountains, van Meurs complained of a chill. They went to the Grand Hôtel des Alpes, a rambling wooden structure of the kind often found during the nineteenth century in obscure places for the accommodation of adventuresome travelers. The following day was a Sunday. Rain was falling on the mountainsides, on the somber forest, and dripping from the balconies of the hotel. Van Meurs awoke unwell and in severe pain. Complaining of kidney stones, he writhed from side to side on his bed, banging his head repeatedly against the wall. Alarmed, Alberto called for assistance and found that the hotel luckily had a doctor attached to its staff, as accidents were frequent among mountain climbers. He examined van Meurs and gave him an injection to ease the pain. Alberto remained by the bedside of the elderly Dutchman. Having brought with him a copy of Flaubert's *Bouvard et Pécuchet*, he began to read the introductory essay by Guy de Maupassant. In it there is a passage which cannot have failed to impress the suggestible young artist as he sat by the bedside of this sick man who was, in effect, a stranger. Speaking of Flaubert, Maupassant observes:

> Those people who are altogether happy, strong, and healthy: are they adequately prepared to understand, to penetrate, and to express this life we live, so tormented, so short? Are they made, the exuberant and outgoing, for the discovery of all those afflictions and all those sufferings which beset us, for the knowledge that death strikes without surcease, every day and everywhere, ferocious, blind, fatal? So it is possible, it is probable, that the first seizure of epilepsy made a deep mark of melancholy and fear upon the mind of this robust youth. It is probable that thereafter a kind of apprehension toward life remained with him, a manner somewhat more somber of considering things, a suspicion of outward events, a mistrust of apparent happiness.

Under very singular circumstances at a highly vulnerable time of life was it entirely by chance that Alberto Giacometti found these sentences before his eyes? Is it possible to accept as coincidence the nearly supernatural pertinence of such words to the whole future of Alberto's existence? Coincidence very cleverly conceals purpose and compliance, while chance is the convenient hiding place of predetermination.

Rain continued to fall on the mountains and the hotel. Van Meurs showed no signs of improving. On the contrary. His cheeks had become sunken, and he was barely breathing through his open mouth. Alberto took paper and pencil to draw the sick man: to see him more clearly, to try to grasp and hold the sight before his eyes, to understand it, to make something permanent of the passing moment. He drew the sunken cheeks, the open mouth, and the fleshy nose which even as he watched seemed bizarrely to grow longer and longer. Suddenly it occurred to him that van Meurs was going to die, and he was seized by blind fear. The doctor returned toward twilight, examined the patient, then took Alberto aside and said, "It's finished. The heart's failing. Tonight he'll be dead. There's nothing to be done."

Alberto waited by the bedside of the dying man. Nightfall came. Hours passed. Peter van Meurs died.

In that instant, everything changed for Alberto Giacometti forever. He said so, and never ceased saying so. The subsequent testimony of his lifetime showed that it was the truth. Till then, he said, he had had no idea, no inkling of what death was. He had thought of life as possessing a force, a persistence, a permanence all its own, and of death as a final occurrence which might somehow enhance the solemnity, and even the value, of life. Now death was immediately present before his eyes with a power which reduced life to nothingness. He had witnessed the transition of being to nonbeing. What had once seemed valuable and solemn was now visibly absurd and trivial. He had seen that life is frail, uncertain, transitory.

> When I saw how that could happen [he wrote later], at the very instant when I saw how that person died, everything was threatened. For me it was like an abominable trap. In a few hours van Meurs had become an object, nothing. Then death became possible at every moment for me, for everyone. It was like a warning. So much had come about by chance: the train, the meeting, the advertisement. As if everything had been prepared to make me witness this wretched end. My whole life certainly shifted in one stroke on that day. Everything became fragile for me.

Alberto, at least, glimpsed the likelihood of predestination and the suggestion of warning. He perceived the abrupt and vital shift of his life to come, but he had no inkling of the reason, for that would truly have been unbearable. He maintained that he previously had had no notion of what death was. This was untrue. His beloved grandfather, to whom he had been very close, died when he was twelve, and family mourning was taken very seriously. And only one year before, a favorite teacher at Schiers had died suddenly. Death was not new to him. But this one was profoundly different.

That night Alberto did not rest well. He did not dare to sleep for fear he might never waken. He was also afraid of the dark, as if the extinction of light were the extinction of life, as if the loss of sight would entail the loss of everything. All night, he kept the light burning by his bedside. He shook himself repeatedly, trying not to sleep, and remained awake till dawn. His first impulse was to flee from Madonna di Campiglio, to escape the scene of sudden death, the sense of fate, to forget what had happened, to return to the security and innocence of his former life. But it was too late. If he did not fully understand what had happened, he understood, at least, that he would never rediscover the simplicity and delight of his youth. That this was the case was dramatically demonstrated in the morning.

It seemed that there might be something suspicious about the circumstances of the Dutchman's death. The doctor was categorical as to heart failure, but a strange inflammation had been found on the dead man's chest. Further examination would be required. Meanwhile, police were summoned from Trento in the valley below and Alberto was placed under guard. To be sure, the authorities may only have feared that van Meurs might have borne some seriously contagious malady and wished, if so, that his young traveling companion should have no opportunity to spread it. Perhaps they entertained other doubts. That a sixty-one-year-old Dutchman should have been traveling about in a remote area with a nineteen-year-old Swiss-Italian youth whom he knew barely at all cannot have failed to rouse curiosity and, indeed, suspicion, for such queer semblances of companionship were only too familiar to the Italian police. For Alberto, in any case, after the sleeplessness and terror of the preceding night, to find himself in the custody of the police | 41 was surely further disquiet, for detention by the police always smacks of crime and imputes guilt.

Now we must confront the most ambiguous and inconclusive issue relating to van Meurs in this entire, exceedingly enigmatic, experience: Did or did he not make physical, explicitly sexual advances toward his youthful companion before falling ill? Trivial corroborative arguments are far from conclusive but deserve a hearing. Van Meurs personally, if we may reasonably take his homosexuality for granted, had a good deal at stake, having gone to considerable trouble, incurred some expense, and, most particularly, having so tenaciously desired to procure the companionship of this specific youth and no other. It strains credulity to conclude that such an opportunity might have been contrived without design. I do not mean to propose speculation as proof. Verification would come in its own fateful time, and it was Alberto himself—without ever needing to be specific—who provided it in abundance for the rest of his life. Even a hesitant, tentative advance would have been felt to constitute a provocation, an overt aggression on the part of a virtual stranger encountered by chance, and it was precisely to such aggression that a robust young man would want to react even should this entail a lifelong effect.

Examination disclosed that van Meurs had died, as predicted, solely of heart failure. Having spent a night in police custody, Alberto was free to go. Instead of returning directly home, however, he decided—"in spite of everything," he said—to go on to Venice, the destination planned from the beginning. The day after his arrival he sent a postcard to his parents, assuring them that Venice was more agreeable than ever, an enchantment, "where one heard singing and whistling all day long," and adding, "the bad memories are fading away." But it was not so. Instead of hurrying from church to church in worship of Tintoretto, he ran after prostitutes and spent his time in cafés. One evening, to his surprise, he found himself racing through the confining alleyways of the city, along obscure canals, across out-of-the-way squares, clutching in one hand a piece of bread of which he longed to rid himself. "I went through all of Venice," he wrote many years later, "looking for remote and lonely neighborhoods, and there, after several unsuccessful attempts on the darkest little bridges and along the most somber canals, trembling nervously, I threw the bread into the stinking water at the dead end of a canal enclosed by dark walls, and I rushed away in a panic, hardly conscious of myself."

Consciousness, however, existed, though he could hardly be, and was not meant to be, familiar with it. That was the cause of his panic, the nervous agitation and overpowering need to rid himself of the piece of bread. "The staff of life" was now the very stuff of life. Witness to a compulsion fatefully different from that which had made it vitally desirable in the depths of his beloved cave. But he could not throw away what had happened. Bread could have filled the canals of Venice to overflowing, but a ritual act could not grant the deliverance he sought. It would have to spring from confrontation with the truth. He certainly lived for it, but to assume as a verity that he recognized the | 43 death of van Meurs as a symbolic, albeit unknow-ing, act of parricide would be asking too much. And yet the structure of his life, as he himself asserted, "shifted on one stroke on that day." It would, of course, be highly tendentious to consider Alberto in any way responsible for van Meurs's end, but respon-sibility is not consonant with a sense of guilt. Had he not agreed to accompany a total stranger to the cross-roads of death, then van Meurs might very plausibly have lived on in Holland and not died in the Italian wilderness.

On his return home he talked tirelessly of what had happened. Indeed, he talked of it tirelessly for the rest of his life. Nor was talk the only lifelong reaction to this experience which, as if by deliberation, he had brought upon himself. Not only did Alberto continue to arrange his socks and shoes with the same previous precision before retiring, but now he had acquired an-other nocturnal obsession. He refused to sleep with-out a light burning throughout the night beside his bed. "It's childish, of course," he readily acknowledged. "I know perfectly well that one is no more threatened in the dark than in broad daylight." Still, the light re-mained burning, wherever the bedroom happened to be, and whatever the circumstances, for the next forty-four years and four months. It was symptomatic of anxiety, and where there is anxiety there must be something of which one is afraid. What had hap-pened at Madonna di Campiglio had happened in re-ality, not in the fantasy of a child or the dream of a grown man. The true emotion, it seems, roused in
children when they are left in the dark is not dread

but desire, an overwhelming and fearful longing for the only one who can bring solace for an apparent loss of self in the visible world. The light becomes both a beacon and a being, a summons and a response, illuminating the darkness that is prelude to sleep, which itself is next door to the next world. Thus, Alberto symbolically introduced his mother to the event at Madonna di Campiglio, introduced himself, so to speak, to her herself more intimately than ever before, and on the eve of his twentieth birthday set about confronting the destiny which would make him a great artist and a great man.

The cane which Alberto had carried with such pride in Rome, tapping it constantly around him, "always endangering someone's life," as he (humorously?) remarked, did not seem appropriate in Stampa. Nor did the fine clothes of which he had formerly been so proud. His period of sartorial self-satisfaction had been brief. He never again showed any interest in smart attire. In fact, it sometimes seemed that he went out of his way to appear shabby.

A decision was taken as to Alberto's professional future. He would receive a parental subsidy, travel to Paris, and enter the class of Antoine Bourdelle, a well-known sculptor, at the Académie de la Grande-Chaumière. On the twenty-eighth of December 1921, the young man left Stampa, traveling by way of Zurich to Basel, where he would be obliged to obtain a visa for entry into France. Formalities, plus the New Year holiday, delayed delivery of the visa. Two nights before his departure, he dreamed that he was already in the train, that everything was beautiful and the railway cars of fabulous size. On the evening of January 8, 1922, his dream came true. Traveling alone, Alberto crossed the border from Switzerland to France for the first time. As the night train rolled westward through the Vosges, perhaps its railway cars did not seem so fabulous after all. But their destination was.

Giacometti stated invariably in later years that he had arrived in Paris for the first time on New Year's Day 1922. Documents, however, confirm that he arrived on January 9. The inaccuracy has persisted and to this day is accepted as correct in catalogue prefaces and countless monographs. It is intriguing, because at first it seems so pointless. To arrive for the first time in Paris in 1922 was without exaggeration a momentous event for a young artist aged twenty. If his arrival happened to coincide with the very first day of a new year, the coincidence might reasonably have impressed him as a favorable augury. But if he did not arrive on that day, then neither impression nor augury could logically have been taken for granted. By insisting all his life that he had arrived on the very first day, Alberto once again was taking his destiny into his own hands, demonstrating a disposition to live with experience in such a way that a mythical imperative can take precedence over mere fact.

The Sphinx was unquestionably ascendant when Alberto first arrived in Paris. It was not a creature, however, but a place; a place, moreover, which presented the challenge of beings who did not necessarily have to be considered as persons. But it was precisely this place which provided for Alberto the answer to the riddle of every man's lifetime. He responded to its challenge with passion, for the Sphinx was the city's most famous brothel. It stood at 31, boulevard Edgar-Quinet, behind the Montparnasse railway station. "For me it was a place more marvelous than any other," Alberto said. This was doubtless so, because there he found a pragmatic answer to the riddle of existence which for him was fundamental: the enigma of viable manhood. Alberto's feelings toward women were profoundly ambivalent. He both adored and abhorred them. From an early age, attentive to fantasies of violence, he had conceived of the sexual act not only as cold and mechanical but also as a combat. "I always felt very deficient sexually," he said. The reason was not physiological, however. Though the mumps had made him sterile, he was perfectly capable of sexual intercourse. And yet he never felt sure of achieving satisfactory completion of the act, no matter how fiercely he desired it. This sense of sexual inhibition, though, did not occur equally with all women. By a convenient but logical process of selectivity, whores were exempt. Alberto's partiality to prostitutes had become increasingly pronounced since his first experience in Rome, and it was confirmed in Paris as a lifelong proclivity. "Whores are the most honest of girls," he said. "They present the bill right away. The others hang on and never let you go. When one lives with problems of impotence, the prostitute is ideal. You pay, and whether or not you fail is of no importance. She doesn't care." The Sphinx never put him to a test which he need fear and provided him with a knowing opportunity to believe in his response to the mystery of his own being. He lived with the problems of impotence, to be sure, but they were sexual only in their practical application, so to speak. A prostitute seemed to be ideal not because she relieved the discomfort and indignity of impotence but because the character of relations with her concealed the true ideal of womanhood Alberto revered. Thus, in terms of the conflict which he believed to exist between men and women, he was running away from reality no less than he had wanted to run away from the fearful experience at Madonna di Campiglio. And consistent with his concept of relations between men and women as combat, he spoke of marriage as surrender and was sternly hostile to the idea and institution—with a single inspiring exception, of course: the person to whom he owed his life and his own creative development.

It was not until 1927, having by that time executed numerous portraits of his mother, which he continued to do as long as she lived, that Alberto finally undertook to portray his father in a series of surprising, interesting sculptures that demonstrate his evolution toward an original style which was frankly displeasing to Giovanni. The first in the series is a highly skilled academic likeness, suggesting an effort by the artist to please, if not to flatter, his model. The effort failed, for it offers only an appearance, not the conviction, of life. It was followed, however, by others, which grew gradually more distorted and abstract until resemblance to Giovanni had vanished and there remained but the work of art itself. The front of the head grew flatter and flatter. In one version it is a completely flat plane on which the recognizable but distorted features of the model are carelessly scratched—almost as an afterthought—and are, in any case, irrelevant to the validity of the sculptural object. A version in white marble is so close to abstraction that it is identifiable only because the roughly triangular shape of the face is similar to the completely flat "portrait." Finally, there is a small sculpture which is in fact but a mask and represents the father's features as a violent, almost brutal caricature. What Giovanni can have felt about these supposed likenesses one may surmise, because they seem deliberately conceived to annihilate the aesthetic vision to which he had devoted his own life. What Alberto may have imagined he was actually up to when taking it upon himself to execute these unlikely works is so ambivalent as to be troubling. And yet such was the outward affection and harmony between father and son that no open malaise ever came between them.

Alberto, lively, sociable, a brilliant and original conversationalist, had many friends among the artists, writers, and bohemians who flocked to Montparnasse. One evening early in April of 1932, both he and his brother Diego were at the Café du Dôme, seated, as was often the case, with different people at different tables. Diego did not like the look of his brother's companions. There were four men and two women.

The poet Tristan Tzara, founder of Dada, was one. The others were Jacques Cottance and Georges Weinstein, two young acolytes of the Surrealist movement, and a handsome artist of twenty-three named Robert Jourdan. The women were two sisters, Denise and Colette Bellon. It appeared to be a lively group out for an evening of drink and talk, nothing more. But Diego did not feel reassured. Always early to bed, he returned to his ramshackle, spartan lodging in the rue d'Alésia. His sleep was troubled by a dream in which he saw Alberto struggling half-submerged, in a black, slimy morass from which he could not escape, while Diego, at a distance, powerless to help, could only look on with dismay. At the Dôme, in the meantime, Cottance and Weinstein had also absented themselves. The talk turned to drugs, as young Jourdan was addicted to opium. His father was a high official in the Department of the Seine, and Robert, still living at home, could hardly indulge his habit on the parental premises. He suggested to his friends that they go somewhere and take dross, the gummy substance left over after opium has been smoked. He had plenty of it with him. They agreed. Denise Bellon, living in a small apartment in a pension in the rue Faustin-Hélie, offered her place for the party, and the five set off by taxi. Tzara, always canny, begged off at the last minute, leaving Denise, Colette, Alberto, and Robert to go upstairs together. The dross was produced and consumed. Whether pleasurable or merely stupefying, the effects were soon felt. Everybody drowsed. Toward morning, Alberto came to himself, lying fully clothed on a bed. He slowly realized where he was and remembered what had happened. It was not yet daylight. Beside him lay Robert. The two young women reposed somewhere nearby. Gradually Alberto became more conscious of his surroundings. Robert lay still, so still that it seemed he could hardly be breathing. He was *not* breathing. Alberto turned violently on the bed. Robert's body was no longer warm. It lay there with a terrifying stillness, cold, dead. Once again, suddenly, unaccountably, Alberto found himself in a strange room at night beside a corpse. Once again, as in the rainy mountains of northern Italy, chance had brought him face-to-face with death. Had some predestination, perhaps, again lain in wait to take the measure of his resolve to scrutinize the truth about himself? He had never before taken drugs, never took them again. His instant impulse, as at Madonna di Campiglio, was to flee. Getting up from the bed where the dead man lay, he went quickly to the door and hurried down to the street. It was cold and raining. He found a taxi and returned to his studio. But the police, of course, had to be called. When they heard what had happened, a van was sent to bring the fugitive witness to the station at 2, rue Bois-le-Vent. So it was that Alberto once again found himself detained by the authorities because of a death in which his involvement seemed to have been accidental. If detainment by the police entails a sense of guilt, however, the extent of its presumption need not derive from a rational appraisal of the facts. He had now kept a light burning at night by his bedside for eleven years, but it had averted nothing. The formalities at the police station, like those in Italy, proved to be no more than formalities. It was clear that Jourdan had died of an overdose, and the dead boy's influential father managed to suppress all reference to this scandalous fact. The witnesses were released, no report was prepared, and the death certificate, omitting to state a cause, was issued after the funeral had taken place. When Diego learned what had happened, he was understandably upset. The coincidence of his dream with Alberto's experience, though subject to more complex interpretations than he could have been expected to make, surely increased his disposition to feel that Alberto needed help and protection, most of all from himself. This can hardly be counted in the score of chance. It may be valid, moreover, to mention that Alberto, despite his uncompromising candor, never spoke of Robert Jourdan's death. I learned of it entirely by accident from the daughter of one of the young women present, with whom I had no reason to speak of Giacometti; later Diego, less forthcoming than his brother, and astonished that I had learned of the long-past incident, reluctantly confirmed the facts and told me of his dream.

The last portrait undertaken by Alberto of his father was a painting, not a sculpture, executed in 1932. Giovanni was then but sixty-four years old. The full-face portrait is of a man who looks much older, old before his time, wistful, weary, nearly bald, his gaze

fixed upon some indecipherable remoteness, lips

pressed tight in an expression of melancholy withdrawal, altogether an image of exhausted resignation. Whether or not this portrait is a reliable likeness one cannot judge, but it does reveal how the son saw his father at the precise age when he himself, thirty-two years later, was destined to die. As a matter of fact, Giovanni was indeed weary. A doctor of his acquaintance named Widmer, a collector of his paintings, who owned a sanatorium at Glion in the mountains above Montreux, invited the tired artist to come there for a rest. Giovanni was pleased to accept and went to Glion in the late spring of 1933. A rest, however, was all that seemed necessary. Dr. Widmer assured Annetta that there was no reason to worry. After a short time, feeling improved, Giovanni asked his wife to go to Maloja and open the summer house where they spent their vacations. All seemed well, but on the twenty-third of June the artist suffered a cerebral hemorrhage and lapsed into a coma. Annetta hurried back from Maloja, Bruno from Zurich, Ottilia from Geneva. They arrived the following day. Though the patient remained unconscious, there appeared to be no immediate danger. Hoping for prompt improvement, it was decided not to alert Alberto and Diego yet.

The next day was a Sunday. Rain was falling on the mountainside, on the forests, on the fields around the sanatorium. At the bedside of the sick man, Annetta, her daughter, and her youngest son waited, and as the hours passed, it became clear that Giovanni, still unconscious, was dying. Bruno notified his brothers in Paris. No such convenience as a telephone existed | 53 in the studio, but the message got through. They took the night train from the Gare de Lyon. Alberto felt unwell as the train rolled eastward toward Switzerland. His malaise was an indefinite feeling of infirmity and fatigue rather than a specific identifiable symptom of illness. He cannot have been in doubt concerning what awaited him in the rainy mountains above Montreux. Bruno was at the station in the morning. He told his brothers at once that their father had died during the night. Then the three of them drove together up into the mountains. It was still raining. At the clinic they were met by Annetta and Ottilia, then all five together, the mother, her daughter, and three sons, went to the room where Giovanni Giacometti, their husband and father, lay dead. For some time they stood in silent reverence before the corpse. Very shortly, however, Alberto announced that he felt indisposed and feverish and would have to go to bed. A nearby room was available and Dr. Widmer made an examination. It disclosed that the young man did, indeed, have a fever, though this was due to no discernible infection or malady. Rest seemed the only sensible prescription. Alberto concurred and remained in bed.

More practical and less emotional than his brothers, Bruno made the arrangements for removal of the dead artist's remains to Stampa, for the funeral and interment in the nearby churchyard of San Giorgio at Borgonovo, where Giovanni's father and many relations already lay. The death of Giovanni Giacometti was an event of national importance. Newspapers were prompt to publish eulogistic accounts of the artist's career, and his passing was rightly noted as a loss to the cultural life of the country. The family was notified that a government representative would be present at the formal ceremony. While Alberto remained in bed, Bruno went several times to his room to consult with him about the arrangements. The older brother would have no part in them. Lying rigidly outstretched beneath the bedclothes, he would not even respond. This adamant refusal to participate in any way in an event of capital significance to the family was surprising, even troubling, especially since the eldest son by tradition assumed the authority of the father upon the latter's death. It could only be assumed that Alberto's inexplicable illness was responsible for his untoward behavior. The following day, the family prepared to leave Glion to accompany homeward Giovanni's remains. Alberto insisted that he was as yet too ill to travel. The others had no choice but to go on as planned. He would join them as soon as he felt physically able. This, it turned out, was not for a number of days, with the result that he did not arrive in time for Giovanni's funeral. So Alberto was not present to honor the artist or make a son's final gesture of piety and devotion, remaining apart from the central figures of his life, who were busy performing the rites appropriate to one of its crucial events. Why? It is one of the paramount questions in his life and decisive for his evolution as an artist. This time there were no police, there was no bread, no staff of life to be coped with, no absence of the bedside light, no trouble in arranging socks and shoes. The corpse he'd had to confront was not that of a stranger. His malady, which had nothing to do with bodily disease or injury, was nonetheless a malady as grave as any that he might contract. He would not, he *could* not take his father's place as head of the family. By his fault, which had been merely his presence, a symbolic father, a stranger encountered by chance, had already died a dozen years before. And as he lay safely in his hospital bed, the infection of guilt was a truly explicable malady.

In time, of course, the fever subsided. Alberto traveled home, restored, apparently, both to his family and to himself after the mysterious malady. However, he chose not to remain for long away from Paris, where urgent work, he said, required his presence. Yet what this work may have been we do not know, as he produced almost nothing during the remainder of the year. The first six months of 1933, in fact, had already indicated a weakening of the artist's commitment to Surrealism, and in 1934 he executed but a single sculpture which could be described, allowing for some latitude, as Surrealist. Thus, the end of Alberto's so-called Surrealist period, of which his father had disapproved, appears for all intents and profound purposes to have coincided with Giovanni's death.

Before saying too definitive a farewell to Alberto's Surrealism, however, it may be apposite to speak in particular of one work among the many that represent sexual violence, cruelty, and death. In *Point to the Eye*, a club-shaped form tapering to a stiletto point is thrust across a barren space directly toward the eye socket in the skull-like head of a stylized skeleton; thrusts but does not quite touch, threatens but does not quite pierce, and so the expressive sense of the sculpture is one of deadly menace. For an artist, vision is equivalent to life, and the natural result of their union is a work of art. Creation is procreation. To be blinded is to lose creative power, to be made impotent in a way which goes beyond artistic capacity, to have met with a living death. Alberto's psyche worked upon him, and upon his art, with relentless subtlety. To have seen so acutely and with such unflinching penetration so far into the symbolic future called for courage and clairvoyance of extreme audacity, which is the point—maddeningly rare and indescribably precious—of all art representing subject matter that defies the resources of representation.

One year after his father's death, Alberto executed a design for Giovanni's tombstone. The decision was his own. He was the eldest son, a sculptor. What would be more natural than for filial gratitude and piety to find expression in a tangible and enduring memorial? Working from his brother's design, the funerary monument was carved from a boulder of local stone by Diego—Alberto never cared for the labor of working with stone—and it is sober, discreet, impressive. Above the name of the dead artist appear in low relief a bird, a chalice, a sun, and a star. A bird with a chalice is symbolic of the certainty of eternal life, while sun and star are age-old symbols of rebirth and return. This would have seemed the very least an understanding son might hope to do. In later years, whenever Alberto spoke of his father, and he spoke of him often, it was invariably with particular insistence upon his gentle kindness, generosity, tolerance, and talent. Never once to my knowledge did he refer to the malady which had confined him to a sickroom while the paternal memory and achievements were being honored in a distant cemetery. I only learned of this from Bruno, who spoke of it with reluctance and puzzlement forty-five years later.

Alberto's emotional impulses and physical desires had not provided him with an enduring attachment, which he did not crave, or even a relationship that could very well qualify as a love affair. Prostitutes continued to be the abiding solution to the insoluble problem. "When I'm walking along the street and see from a distance a whore all dressed," he said, "I see a whore. When she is in the room standing naked before me, I see a goddess." Alberto's vision of the prostitute as goddess was to have a decisive influence on his art. It was not long after his definitive break with Surrealism that he made the acquaintance of a woman unlike any other he had ever known, or was ever to know, not a prostitute specifically but a woman of many affairs, exotic allure, and remarkable sexual exuberance. Her name was Isabel Nicholas, and it seems plausible to assume that no other woman made more telling a mark on Alberto's life. Alberto called her "a devourer of men." Exceptionally beautiful, with a fierce, animal confidence in her right to do as she pleased, she participated in life with a zest that made her company exciting and meaningful for women as well as for men. English by birth, married to a foreign correspondent, she frequented Montparnasse as a regular, picturesque, hilarious fixture. Alberto was strongly attracted to her from the first but made his advances with caution, as if a close rapport might entail some danger, and it so happens that the purposeful postponement of immediate gratification of sexual desires allows more valuable purposes to be fulfilled. On October 10, 1938, Giacometti celebrated his thirty-seventh birthday. More than half his lifetime had already passed. One of its critical events was to occur just eight days later. Isabel was crucially implicated. Alberto had judged her potential effect with oracular acumen, for the manner in which he would make his way through life and through the world would be changed forever.

The afternoon was cloudy and cool. Isabel had come to Alberto's studio to pose. While she remained motionless, he walked back and forth, observing her. "Look how well one can walk with both legs," he remarked. "Isn't it wonderful? Perfect equilibrium." However, his sense of inner equilibrium was neither confident nor marvelous. Isabel was there before him, yielding to the artist's gaze, but to the man she remained remote and intimidating. He still did not know where he stood with her. Their relationship had been more or less close for nearly three years, yet nothing had come of it. He was in love with her, but they were not lovers. To be sure, this was his own fault, as he could not bring himself to make overt gestures or commitments. That evening they went to dinner, afterward meeting friends at St.-Germain-des-Prés. Isabel decided to return to her hotel toward midnight, and Alberto accompanied her on foot. As they walked, he felt that the inconclusiveness of relations had become so demoralizing that he should break with her once and for all. Trying to explain his feelings, he said, "I've absolutely lost my footing." To walk from St.-Germain-des-Prés to the rue St.-Roch, where Isabel's hotel was located, cannot have taken more than twenty minutes. This interlude did not lead to the consummation for which Alberto wished, for at the door to Isabel's hotel, he was unable to make the advances which would surely have led him upstairs to her room and into her bed. But he could not bring himself, either, to make a definite break. As he turned away in the chilly dark, it must have seemed that his predicament was virtually crippling, and in view of what was shortly to occur it will be enlightening to recall not only that the circumstances were the consequence of sexual inhibition and frustration but also that accidents are famously resourceful in concealing a purpose.

At its southern end, the rue St.-Roch gives into the rue de Rivoli. Turning left under the arcade, Alberto came to the Place des Pyramides, a small square created by Napoleon to commemorate his brilliant victory over the Mameluks. In its center on a high pedestal stands the equestrian statue of another famous forger of French destiny, Joan of Arc. Round the base of the pedestal is an oval sidewalk barely six feet wide. It was to this spot, charged with such a variety of associations, that Alberto came in the middle of that October night. And suddenly an automobile came speeding along the rue de Rivoli, swerved toward him, careened onto the narrow width of sidewalk, and knocked him down. The car hurtled onward beneath the arcade and smashed through a shop window. Alberto lay on the pavement, surprised but calm, aware that something was wrong with his right foot and that his shoe lay to one side. People came running. A police van arrived, siren blaring. Alberto retrieved his shoe, and his foot began to hurt. The driver of the car, extricated from the wreck, turned out to be a woman, an American. Alberto thought she was half-crazy, a prostitute. Though he wanted only to go home, the police—the police yet again, and not for the last time—insisted he be taken with the woman to the emergency room of the Bichat Hospital to see whether either had sustained serious injury. The woman turned out to have been drunk and was released into the custody of the police. Nothing further was ever heard of her, and relevant records have not survived. Anyway, she had served her purpose. Alberto's foot was seriously swollen and he was placed in a ward to await examination the next morning.

Diego and influential friends of both brothers arranged to have Alberto promptly transferred from the public hospital to the private Rémy de Gourmont Clinic, presided over by one of Paris's most eminent surgeons, Dr. Raymond Leibovici. X-ray examination revealed that the metatarsal arch of Alberto's right foot was broken at two points, but the displacement was not so severe as to require surgery. A plaster cast would be quite sufficient to ensure normal healing of the breaks once the bones had been set in their proper alignment, and within ten or twelve weeks the injury would be entirely healed, leaving no lasting disability. Accordingly the broken bones were set and a first cast applied without complication. By the next day the patient was feeling well, rested, eating with appetite, very pleased with the clinic and its good-looking nurses. But Alberto was worried about his mother. Always anxious to protect her from knowledge that might be troubling, he took care to assure her that the accident was not grave.

Alberto was obliged to remain at the clinic until the swelling of his foot had subsided and a more durable cast could be applied. When Isabel learned of his whereabouts, she came immediately to visit, and as if by some supernatural intervention Alberto no longer felt tormented by the relationship. The elusive, menacing aspect of Isabel's person and presence henceforth ceased to cause him anxiety, and it was the injury to his foot that made all the difference. If he knew why, he did not explain. Nor was an explanation necessary, after all, because it dwelt autonomously in the difference. With some insistence Alberto declared, "I feel better than before this adventure." Being closer to the truth, his statement needed more explanation than the difference itself. After one week in the hospital, when the first cast was removed and replaced by a heavier one, Dr. Leibovici sent his patient home, assuring him again that there would be no aftereffects.

Walking with crutches, Alberto found, was a lark, like having four legs instead of two, and he delighted in experimenting with a novel sense of equilibrium and an altered view of his situation in space. An altered view is a vital transformation of physical, psychic, and aesthetic interrelations for one to whom

visual relations with the world are paramount. The injury to his foot offered a benefit not only to his emotional life but also to his creative activity. He happily and repeatedly told his friends that being lame was the best thing that could have happened to him as an artist. He may have felt that the continued use of crutches would give longevity to the benefit. The crutches pointed to the sense of it, which was important, and what was most important to Alberto was his work. A month after the second plaster cast had been applied, it was removed. Dr. Leibovici was pleased to find his prognosis confirmed. The bones had knit perfectly. Some swelling and stiffness remained, but these would disappear completely after some weeks of massage and muscular reeducation. Alberto would have to remain on crutches for a time. Its length depended on him, on the regularity and conscientiousness with which he undertook physical therapy. Dr. Leibovici discharged his patient with the conviction of having served him well. In any event, they were not to meet again for twenty-five years.

Despite his doctor's prediction, Alberto kept to his crutches. Never one to watch his step when it came to his health, he repeatedly put off the essential therapy. This delay may have been due in part to his enjoyment of walking with the crutches. Maybe the enjoyment was a symptom of a more fundamental causality. Time would tell. Meanwhile, there was work of enhanced importance to be done, and the fact that he was lame was no reason to put it off. On the contrary. Since his abandonment of Surrealism, Alberto had spent his energy on representational works, principally portrait busts of Diego and another model, a woman. After the "accident," however, he began a series of female figures modeled from memory, and these brought a radical difficulty into his life and work. He wanted to renew his vision, to see what stood before him with the original, vital freshness of a child, a child who long ago felt he could reproduce and possess whatever he wanted with the simple weapon of a pencil. But it was not so simple now. Critical complexities had intervened. The sculptures on which he labored dwindled and dwindled between his fingers, growing so tiny from his painstaking efforts that they often crumbled into dust. His problem had become anthropological. Having determined to make a new beginning in his own art, and in art altogether, as though art had never existed, he found his hands at grips with works which evoked the origins of creativity, its mysteries and rites. For primitive man, sculpture, unlike painting, was a matter of life and death. Alberto's tiny figurines have something of the talisman, charged with anthropomorphic vitality and magical feeling, as in the Gravettian carvings of 15,000 B.C. They needed to be seen as inhabitants both of actual space, the space of the knowable and the living, and of metaphysical space, the space of the unknowable and the dead. In short, he was working instinctively with greater and greater determination toward the fulfillment of an undertaking which he could not yet recognize both as his life and his art. The results baffled him, but he was not discouraged. *What* he saw had ceased to be as important as *how* he saw, and therefore the whole purpose of creativity had changed. In the search for a uniquely personal vision, it may eventually seem that the works of art which embody that vision can never be equal to the expressive potential of the aesthetic experience. A search for the absolute entails a clear-eyed recognition that its destination is failure—more specifically, death. In those terms, the principal reason for creating works of art will be to demonstrate the continuing possibility of that which as a basic premise is acknowledged to be impossible. No wonder Alberto could go on working with such constancy and assurance. He had reached the state of mind which was to become the very substance of his fulfillment and make of him a unique figure in the culture of his time.

His mother felt worried. She had learned of the accident after all danger, which had been minimal, was past. But even the hint of a mishap to her firstborn and favorite son distressed her. Meanwhile, Alberto eventually gave up his crutches, replacing them with a cane. Limping noticeably, he talked repeatedly of the reason, as it was his lifelong practice to speak openly and frequently of intimate concerns. No one who knew him well at all can have failed to know what had happened one night in the Italian mountains at Madonna di Campiglio, or on another in the Place des Pyramides. Nor was it long before he began telling his friends, as he told them again and again in later years with drastic revisions of the narrative, how glad he had been when he realized that he would remain permanently lame. He doubtless refrained from sharing his satisfaction with Annetta, however, as he always endeavored to protect her, to conceal from her, indeed, any aspect of his life which he had good reason to believe might prove troubling. When he arrived for his traditional summer sojourn in Switzerland, however, he came with his cane.

In September 1939, the chaos in which the inherent disorder of human life is reflected in its most extreme degree exploded upon the world. When Alberto presented himself to the military authorities in Chur, in eastern Switzerland, he carried his cane and was dismissed as unfit for service. Diego was accepted, however, though his tour of duty in a transport battalion lasted but a few months before he was able, as a permanent resident in France, to return to Paris—to his brother and to Nelly, the mistress with whom he had already been living for several years. Alberto's relationship with Isabel had ceased to be demoralizing since the night in the Place des Pyramides, but it had remained inconclusive. They saw each other regularly, and the intensity of a serious emotional attachment was taken for granted. And yet there was no consummation.

Disaster became imminent when Nazi troops and dive bombers attacked the Low Countries, routed the British at Dunkirk, and advanced toward Paris. Isabel, true to form, seems to have felt that she had nothing to fear from men at war. And yet, as those able to leave did so in ever-increasing numbers, and panic spread through Paris, she decided to take the last train to Bordeaux, where a ship would evacuate her to England. The day before her departure, Alberto visited her hotel. He wished to make drawings of her, and, for the first time, in the nude. And it was then, when the enemy was but thirty miles distant, that he discovered his ability to make the decisive gesture which led to a physical bond between them and marked the beginning of a love affair that would be the most significant of Alberto's life, though for most of its duration they were separated, which may have been essential to their attachment.

As Swiss citizens, Alberto and Diego had nothing to fear from the German occupation of Paris save considerable inconvenience and privation. But there was the matriarch. Two years had passed since she had seen either of her expatriate sons. At least one of them, she insisted, must come to visit her in Geneva, where she was occupied with the upbringing of her four-year-old grandson, whose mother, Annetta's only daughter, had died in childbirth. From the first there was no question about which one of the sons would go. Alberto applied for the necessary permit. He planned to be away for two months, maybe three, and promised when leaving to bring back, on his return, sculptures "of less ridiculous size" than the tiny figurines which, as if by a will of their own, had continued to materialize between his fingertips.

The reunion between mother and son was joyful. Being together again came as a relief as well as a confirmation. Annetta was not one to mince words, however, when something displeased her, and she did not like to see her son still walking with a cane, that symbolic third leg famously connoting old age. She had seen it before, of course, but that had been shortly after the accident. Two years had since passed. Alberto still walked with a slight limp, to be sure, but he | 67 could not have been called lame, even less a cripple, and had no need of the cane. Yet he clung to it. His mother protested. For once he paid no heed. His defiance called for attention, because Annetta's pleasure and satisfaction as a rule had always been paramount. But the cane seemed to insist upon its own necessity as something to which their mutual adoration must defer. Thus, a certain tension between mother and son beset the start of a sojourn that would be unexpectedly long and engender graver problems.

Meanwhile, Alberto wanted to get on with his work and resume a way of life as similar as possible to the one he had left behind in Paris. He could not expect to work in the orderly apartment of his brother-in-law, where Annetta looked after her grandson, nor could he presume to live as he pleased under her indulgent but critical eye. He would have to find a place of his own. The place he soon found was, of course, exactly to his liking. Of the several cheap hotels in Geneva which rented rooms to women who made a profession of entertaining chance acquaintances by the hour, the Hôtel de Rive was the smallest and shabbiest, also the cheapest, being farthest from the area where such acquaintances were made. Cheerless and comfortless as well as disreputable, the Hôtel de Rive was a small, three-storied building, with a homely café on the ground floor, a dozen small rooms crowded above. Access to these was conveniently provided by a back doorway. Alberto's room on the third floor, at the top of a circular stairway, measured ten by thirteen feet. Its sole furnishings were an iron bed in one cor-

ner, a rough wooden table which served as a washstand, a mirrored wardrobe, and a couple of chairs. One toilet and one faucet, supplying cold water only, were located outside in the corridor. No heating facilities existed, with the result that overnight residents in cold weather had to sleep fully dressed, and in the morning the water in pitchers or basins would be frozen. With visionary resourcefulness, Giacometti had contrived to install himself in an abode even smaller and, if possible, less comfortable than the one on the rue Hippolyte-Maindron in Paris. No matter. The physical was definitely not the arena in which his decisive combat was to be waged. He thought of his Swiss accommodations as temporary, in any case, for he expected after a few months to return to France. Having been allowed to leave, however, he found himself unable to obtain permission to return.

No time was wasted before getting to work. Change of scene had not changed the artist's predicament. His figures kept on shrinking, as if by a will to become the least common denominator of the visible. Sack after sack of plaster was hefted up the circular staircase, but neither the size nor the number of acceptable works increased, while the accumulating residue gradually transformed the little room into a bizarre wilderness. Chunks and crumbs and flakes and dust of plaster settled upon every surface, clogged every crevice, filled every crack, seeped through every seam of the room itself and of everything in it, including the man whose efforts had brought into being this weird, ancillary spectacle by which he himself was transformed. His hair, his face, his hands, his clothes were so penetrated with plaster dust that no amount of washing or brushing could eliminate it, and the streets neighboring the Hôtel de Rive bore the ghostly imprints of his footsteps. Alberto became a living image of the interdependence between an artist and his art, and from this period dates not only the physical resemblance which eventually came to identify the sculptor with his sculptures but also the genesis of his legendary reputation as a figure of incorruptible dedication to the toil of creativity.

As months passed, while empty plaster sacks accumulated, producing more and more detritus but, if possible, less and less sculpture, Annetta began to lose heart. Unable to understand, she criticized, conceiving a violent dislike for the tiny figurines. "You don't know how much they displease and trouble me," she said. "Your father never did things like that." Her admonition was beyond her comprehension, of course, which was certainly for the best, because if she had grasped its meaning, the consequences would have been fatefully hurtful. As for Alberto, he knew now exactly where he stood in relation to his father and his father's career. And those tiny figurines which dwelt, as it were, between him and his mother during the war years in Geneva, seemed emblematic of what existed between them always, a bond so powerful that disregard or disapproval could never break it, a barrier so strong that compassion could never overcome it. The power of the bond and the strength of the barrier contributed to the dedication of the artist and the devotion of the son. In the end, dedication and devotion turned out to have been the same thing. Alberto and

70 |

Annetta may never have been so united as when they felt separated by the difficulty to which it seemed that each had brought an irreconcilable difference. The symbolic figurine stands as a kind of memorial, commemorating the need to surpass human limitations.

Alberto Giacometti was not a nobody in wartime Geneva. His reputation as a highly inventive Surrealist sculptor had preceded him, and his challenging personality, coruscating conversation, and ingenious sense of humor soon set him in the center of a group of young artists, writers, and bohemian sybarites who gathered nightly at the Café du Commerce. Around the corner, moreover, local ladies loitered, waiting to make acquaintance in the propitious dark of the blacked-out city. They also frequented several louche bars in the vicinity. And so Alberto was able in dour Calvinist Geneva to resume more or less—and mostly more—the lifestyle he had reluctantly left behind in beloved Paris.

Sometime in the autumn of 1943, when the tide of war had started to turn against the Nazis, a painter friend of Alberto's named Rollier brought along to dinner one evening at the Brasserie Centrale a young girl from the suburbs of Geneva. She was said to be interested in things artistic and to be in revolt against a drab bourgeois upbringing. Her father was a schoolteacher in a modest locality called Grand Saconnex, and her schoolmates had been given to mocking her because she made no secret of her desire to link her life to that of a great man. Slender, with fine dark eyes, dark hair, and a clear complexion, she was pretty and had the awkward charm of one whose eagerness for novelty and excitement had not yet been put to the test of experience. She was just twenty year ld. Alberto was struck at once by the quality of her gaze. As the evening passed, he became intrigued. by the person, and his attention must have quickened when he learned that her name was Annette. She took little part in the conversation, but her presence was neither passive nor indifferent. She had extraordinary cause to be attentive, for her intuition had led her to realize that she had attracted the interest of the most remarkable person present. When the better part of the evening had passed, she said that she would have to leave in order to catch the last bus back to the suburb where she lived with her parents and two brothers. Alberto remarked that if she preferred to stay she could later spend the night with him at the Hôtel de Rive. She elected to stay, but she would have to telephone her mother with an explanation. Alberto accompanied her to the telephone, overheard the conversation, and was impressed by the guile with which a girl so young could tell a convincing lie. At the end of the evening they went off together, and even as they walked away in the darkness, he leaning on his cane and old enough to be her father, she skipping along beside him, followed by the astonishment of their friends, they had unknowingly set out upon the mythic thoroughfare which would lead them together for fifteen years toward the denouement of creative destiny.

Not that Alberto for a moment anticipated the least alteration of his habits. He continued to work as before, and with the same frustrating, mysterious results.

Annette had no idea what the tiny figurines were all about, nor was she particularly concerned to find out. The sculptor, not his sculptures, interested her, and the more she saw of him the more interested she became. For his part, Alberto continued to seek out prostitutes, perversely persuading Annette to accompany him to the bars where they congregated and, if possible, to emulate their behavior. Her lack of aptitude as a beginner much entertained him. "You just don't know how to go about it," he said. Later, unfortunately, she learned, and then, of course, it was too late. In addition there was Isabel, the devourer of men, with whom Alberto continually corresponded throughout the war years and expected to rejoin as soon as the hostilities between nations ceased. For the time being, however, three preoccupations balanced upon his days and nights: his work, his mother, and his mistress. Alberto was sincere, kind; he made an issue of ethical probity. So we may assume that the preeminence of his work was well understood both by Annetta and Annette, no matter what each lady may have thought of it, and that the mother was granted no knowledge of the mistress, while the latter willingly accepted the clandestine character of her affair with the son. He must have believed that Annette realized and accepted the tentative character of their relationship, because he allowed her to come and live with him at the Hôtel de Rive, a move unthinkable had it been accompanied by the slightest intimation of a lasting commitment. Still, young people in love project their temporary feelings into the expectation of an enduring and changeless future. Alberto was in a better position to know this than most people. But he allowed Annette to believe in a relationship which he must have known would lead to a situation he was unprepared to accept. One wonders why. The years of labor in the dusty hotel room had brought neither material nor moral increment. His mother disapproved. Annette may have seemed to him, with her girlish laughter, vitality, and easy acceptance of the discomforts of the Hôtel de Rive, to be a kind of daughter on whom he could imaginatively lean, whose devotion would be comforting as he made his way through the wilderness. Then, of course, there was the magic evocativeness of her name.

Neither intelligent nor cultivated, Annette nonetheless possessed exceptional perseverance, suggestible imagination, and a stubborn resolve to get what she wanted. For the time being she was employed as a secretary by the Red Cross. But Annette was not a career girl. Though brought up to admire material achievements, she never felt that she should devote her life to earning a living. She evidently anticipated that the responsibility of her well-being might be assumed by someone who would never expect her to be a bourgeois housewife, because she spent many office hours leaning over her typewriter wondering whether or not she should marry Alberto. That she looked forward to marriage is not surprising, since the blindness of love can account for any anomaly of vision. What is surprising is that at the same time she questioned the desirability of the match. What is astonishing is the cause of her uncertainty. It was not induced by

the fact that Alberto was so much older than she,

by his apparent lack of prospects, or by his well-advertised aversion to the marital state. She hesitated because he was lame. It was only a foolish concern for appearances, no doubt. Annette was never a lucid analytical person. And yet what she saw as a possible obstacle was precisely what a person of oracular lucidity would have seen. However obscure and latent her perception, it added to her relationship with Alberto a dimension which neither of them could foresee, or control, because it would measure them both by the heartless yardstick of symbolic experience. Alberto's limp, to be sure, was neither pronounced nor disabling, and sometimes, in fact, it was almost imperceptible. It seemed to depend on his state of mind at the moment. Still, he walked with a cane, which seemed sufficient proof that he had been the victim of a serious and authentic accident. He spoke of it often, evoking painful weeks spent in the hospital but emphasizing the benefits he believed his injury had brought. The exaggeration of his account was for the time being, perhaps, what made it so difficult for him to get along without the conspicuous cane.

In one of the pocket notebooks (very difficult to date) which Alberto habitually carried with him he wrote:

> *Alberto lame*
> *Alberto lame*
> *Alberto lame*
> *Alberto lame*
> *Alberto lame*
> *Alberto fool*

He was by no means a fool, nor was he actually lame, and yet to himself he insisted upon it. His insistence calls further attention — if any were needed! — to the condition of his right foot and its symbolic meaning. Should additional emphasis of that meaning seem exaggerated, one can hardly disregard the meaning and emphasis provided by the artist in person, who had, after all, deliberately brought upon himself this condition.

One Tuesday in May 1945, the war in Europe was at an end. Isabel had sent word to Geneva that she would join Alberto in Paris as soon as possible. He replied, saying that for months and months he had waited for the moment when he could tell her that he had "to some extent" finished his work, living with the need to attain "a certain dimension" that dwelt for the time being only in his mind's eye. The ideal dimension, however, cannot have been simply in the size of his figurine and certainly had to do with his own stature as a man and an artist. It was not enough that he should impose order upon the complexity and novelty of his works; he had to order the life of their maker in a way consistent with their existence and meaning. Each day, he asserted, there was a little progress. When measured against the absolute, a hairsbreadth of progress can seem limitless. In this perspective, Alberto's resolve, long since legendary, begins to seem virtually heroic. But there is something more. All that work, that struggle, the solitary confinement and hard labor at a task interminably resumed with no assurance of satisfactory completion: it seems too deliberate, too punishing. But genius, of course, implies an unconditional commitment to truth. Truth in art and truth in life, however, are not the same. But the two must unite in the creative act if it is to have significant consequences, which is to say that a work of art will be "true to life" when its existence, its very form, embodies the truths of the artist's life. A work of art can then serve the ancillary purpose of revealing those truths. The artist himself, though, exists inside his truth: he can see what he is only by seeing what he does. What he does remains eternally potential rather than actual, so that he can truly become himself only by dying. No one knew this better than Alberto. That was one of the sources of his tireless compulsion to work. It was also part of the existential dilemma which made the tiny figurines so elusive and troubling. "If I could only make a single figurine," he said, "that truly represents what I'm seeking, then they could all become immense and portray goddesses." So the measure of their greatness is one of feeling, not size, and by that measure they restored to sculpture something of its traditional monumentality. Thus, those arduous years of privation and anxiety in the Hôtel de Rive, far from having been for nothing, had been for everything.

Isabel arrived in Paris before Alberto did. Diego, too, waited for Alberto to return. But the artist was still detained in Geneva by his determination to create at least one figurine that would ideally represent his conceptual vision. And of course he found himself unable to do it. At last, when the summer had come to an end, he put the few remaining figurines into one of the large kitchen matchboxes that were in common use at the time, packed his cardboard suit-case, said goodbye to his mother, farewell to Annette, and on September 17, 1945, took the night train for Paris. Twenty-three years before, he had departed for the first time toward this destination. It had changed since. The destination, that is, as well as the city. He had changed, too, and the evidence of the change would measure the condition of his heroism.

2

It was an ordinary day, cloudy and none too warm, the day Alberto returned to Paris after the longest absence he ever knew till the final one. He found Diego content and his studio exactly as he had left it three years and eight months before. Isabel was no less eager than he for the chance to gaze into each other's eyes. More than five years had passed since that June day when she and Alberto had said goodbye. She—no more than he—could not have forgotten what had happened that afternoon. It seems clear that both of them had since thought of the future in terms of the possible promise of that moment. To be sure, they had changed. In the first place, physically. Though Isabel was but thirty-three, the sheen had already gone from her beauty. The years of hard drinking had left her face rubious and puffy. As for Alberto, he was a decade older than she and had never been one to care either for his appearance or his health. If anything, neglect was his rule. Deeply incised furrows had already marked his forehead and face. But neither of them was deceived by the physical. They had more significant contingencies to contend with, and these had also been subject to change during the war. The inconclusiveness of their past had been left behind in Geneva. Alberto was no longer the same man who had said good night to Isabel seven years before in an anguish of irresolution at the door to her hotel. Though he still walked with a cane, it was now with a difference, which had been the outcome of all he had done in the meantime, no matter what may have been suggested by deceptive appearances. He asked Isabel to come and live with him. She agreed. This would be the first time he had lived even in a semblance of marital stability, and it was not a situation for which he had any aptitude. Nor had Isabel ever shown much inclination to be a conscientious spouse. However, they had not waited five years for the sake of a dalliance.

Isabel was not the only person who noticed that Alberto had changed. Before the war, it had been evident to everyone that his was a singular and imposing personality, with the assumption of genius thrown in to point up the singularity. After the war, his friends and acquaintances saw at once that something had been added. And they were people whose perception was imposing: Balthus, Miró, Masson, Max Ernst, Breton, Eluard, Leiris, Sartre, and even such eminent elders as Matisse, Picasso, Braque, and Laurens. What they saw was that a special aura now marked Giacometti as a man apart. It was the onset of that massive accretion of creative and spiritual power which gradually revealed that his attainment was of legendary stature. Meanwhile, he never ceased to be the

entertaining, brilliant, much appreciated friend welcomed with affection. Nor did he cease—to his continuing dismay—making figurines that grew tinier and tinier as he worked on them. They had from the first been inspired, he told her, by Isabel. His frustration was not shared by her. She had always been attracted to creative men, whether successful or not. Indeed, a lack of success appeared to satisfy her, especially insofar as her rapacious exuberance might seem to have contributed to it. Alberto, however, was not one ever likely to fall prey to a devourer of men. And Isabel presently left him to take up with someone less indomitable, a young musician named René Leibowitz. Alberto regretted the parting, though she sent letters saying that her fondness for him was unchanged. In the event, the new affair was not durable, but Alberto and Isabel remained friendly always.

One day the artist set aside his cane. He saw this as a great occasion and called it to the attention of his friends. Not that they might have failed to note the difference. But one person only would have shared Alberto's feeling that the relinquishment of that symbolic appendage was, indeed, a great occasion. She dwelt far away in Switzerland, but she was surely pleased and relieved the next time she saw her son, which was to be soon. Our attention and curiosity, however, ask to be enlightened concerning this seemingly trivial event. For years Alberto's cane had insistently pointed to the fulfillment of a predestination. That he was very likely unaware of this only enhances | 81 its reality. Oracular power dwells in effect, not necessarily in understanding. The effect for Alberto was revealed in his work. The happenstance that the abandonment of the cane coincided with the termination of his affair with the "devourer of men" and with a dramatic development of his aesthetic vision is but another circumstance intimating that coincidence can be the instrument of causality.

In Geneva, Annette Arm was unaware of what had occurred in Paris. Although Alberto, on leaving, had expressly told her that she must entertain no further expectations concerning him, that is what she anxiously did, writing long letters pleading to be allowed to join him. It no longer seemed to matter that he was lame. Alberto replied, telling his correspondent that she had better stay where she was. But then, after Isabel had run off with René Leibowitz, he did something utterly preposterous and—unless seen in the perspective of imminent destiny—incomprehensible. He wrote to Annette, asking her to do him a favor, a favor explicable only insofar as it suggested that he was unwittingly disposed to take a step in her direction.

He asked her to send him a pair of shoes. It was a thoughtless and irresponsible thing to do. But perhaps Alberto merely considered it practical. Shoes of decent quality, to be sure, were difficult to come by in postwar Paris. Alberto recalled having seen in a shop window in Geneva a pair especially to his liking. Why he felt Annette to be the right person to provide him with those shoes, when other people on the spot, beginning with his mother, could have done so, we can

only surmise. It may well have had much to do with the likelihood of her being, in fact, the wrong person. He wrote a lengthy, detailed letter, describing exactly the shoes he wanted, that pair and no other, giving his size, the location of the shop, and instructions as to how the parcel should be forwarded to him. Not to be entrusted to the post office, it was to pass from hand to hand, beginning in Geneva with Albert Skira, the publisher, and ending in Paris with a young painter named Roger Montandon. Having followed its appointed itinerary, the parcel was delivered one evening to the rue Hippolyte-Maindron. Alberto excitedly tore open the wrappings. But as soon as he saw what was inside he started shouting and sputtering with anger. These were not the shoes he'd wanted, he cried. Annette was an idiot who would never understand anything about anything and he was a fool to have entrusted so important an errand to her. Rushing outside, he furiously flung the shoes into the garbage bin without even having tried them on. Montandon was astonished. Having been acquainted for several years with Alberto—and Diego—he knew that the Giacomettis were given to occasional fiery but short-lived outbursts of anger, though he had never witnessed one like this. It seemed especially insensate because the sculptor, who had very little money, had not hesitated to throw away an expensive, sorely needed pair of shoes. But the soreness of the need had not proceeded from a realm accessible to common sense. It is fair and pertinent to conjecture that Alberto cared little, if at all, about the shoes per se. What he cared about was what went inside them. Annette was not, in fact, to be blamed for a failure of understanding, nor was he, for that matter, a fool to have entrusted so important an errand to her, because its importance dwelt precisely in providing him with an infuriating opportunity to cast away—as he had cast away the cane—a symbol of what he himself could not entirely understand.

At Easter, 1946, Alberto returned to Geneva for a visit with his mother. She must have been happy to see him walking without a cane. With or without a cane, Annette Arm was happy to greet her erstwhile lover. Whether or not she knew of the altered situation in Paris is irrelevant. What mattered was that the point of view from which Alberto and Annette saw each other had changed, because he now suggested for the first time that she should pose for him. The fact looms large upon the vista of mutual expectations, because it so invited her into his world that when she asked yet again to join him in Paris his assent must have been in the making even before he beheld her as a focus for the creative act. And suddenly the entire geography of Giacometti's life is seen to shift, and one good measure of transformed terrain was Alberto's warning that Annette must not expect his way of life to be altered in any way by her presence. The warning should have been addressed to himself. Maybe he believed that Annette's presence would not change his life. Maybe he believed that it would not change hers. No matter what he believed, the change for both would be absolute and the responsibility, of course, when it came to the truth, would be his.

Annette was thrilled to be in Paris, and particularly to be there with the man she loved, a man, moreover, acknowledged by his peers to be remarkable. Idealistic and romantic, she believed that the proper goal of human life was not truth but happiness. Alberto saw things just the other way round, aware that happiness cannot be found or be genuine without facing the multiple, complex, often sorrowful truths that are essential to wisdom, which is the indispensable basis of authentic and legitimate happiness. But this drastic dichotomy was destined to lie long in wait before doing its worst. In the meantime there were halcyon years to come. As if, indeed, by supernatural intervention, the tiny figurines grew taller and taller, offering of themselves the secret grandeur which had been theirs from the beginning. None like these had ever been seen before, those life-sized, slender, large-footed women. Though vaguely reminiscent of certain Etruscan figurines, they are not derived from them, being far closer in spirit to Egyptian deities. The great religious art of our world has always been concerned with the female principle, and its masterpieces are possessed by a profound stillness, as are Giacometti's. They do not stir or strive. They simply are. The law of their being is to do nothing but be. In ancient Egypt, a sculptor was called "one who keeps alive." His works were created to represent the idea of eternity, detaching both past and future from the flux of time. They were "true" to life in order to reveal the "falsehood" of death. When Alberto was asked by a journalist why he worked with such indefatigable determination, he said, "So as not to die." | 85

He had exhibited nothing for more than a decade. Now the dealers knocked on his door. There were exhibitions. Prices were low, but critical esteem was high and the works sold well. The artist was only forty-six years old. His health was good, though troubled occasionally by one complaint or another, the worst being his ceaseless smoker's cough, which with the years grew more and more racking, seeming sometimes little short of a fatal seizure. His solution for every indisposition was to visit an old friend from the Surrealist years, Dr. Theodore Fraenkel, an incompetent physician but the persistent medic of artists and poets, for whom he habitually prescribed—often gratis—some ineffectual therapy or analgesic and advised his patients to get on with their work. Alberto asked for no better remedy.

Annette, having made the best of squalid lodgings at the Hôtel de Rive, was pleasantly prepared in Paris to suit herself to only slightly better accommodations in the rue Hippolyte-Maindron. These, to be sure, did not include central heating, hot water, a bathroom, a kitchen, or even a private toilet. But such were the privations that satisfied Alberto, and his satisfaction was all that she had followed him to secure for herself. She proved herself quite as willing as his mother, for example, to live without "modern" comforts, aware that the practical inconveniences of Alberto's lodgings in the rue Hippolyte-Maindron were hardly more extreme than those familiar to the frugal matriarch of Stampa, where Annetta often sat in the dark after nightfall to spare electricity. Annette was eager to do the same. It had become her responsibility, and her right. To this end she was ready to do all she could, and she did much. She happily put up not only with the material hardships of daily life but also with those, far more exacting, of posing constantly for her lover, often naked, remaining rigidly immobile for hours at a time. That punishing routine made critical demands upon her physical and emotional stamina, but she courageously accepted them, because they contributed to the artist's importance, which was essential to her own. She knew that. However, she had no inkling that his importance was of a sort to which she could never hope to accede, even less, indeed, to comprehend. All the same, Alberto accepted her as she was and installed her in the midst of his life. In Paris, that is, not in Stampa, where Annetta would never have welcomed her. But Jean-Paul Sartre, Simone de Beauvoir, Balthus, Lacan, and Alberto's other friends in Paris, where he knew everybody, greeted her tolerantly enough. She may have contributed little to their brilliant, imposing conversations, yet there she was, accepted by all as the artist's mistress, and their acceptance, not to mention his own, presently gave her ideas. Being the mistress of a man promised to greatness was all very well, but being his wife would be infinitely better, offering her a fair share of the great promise thus consecrated by marital vows.

It should have been unthinkable. But Annette didn't think. Her emotions were all of her intellect, their claim for satisfaction her commitment to the truths of life altogether. The grounds for union were, consequently, shaky. Alberto knew that the maker of decisions must accept responsibility for them. And he knew that nobody is ever entirely free to make choices, to measure the prospects of satisfaction, or to judge accurately the wisdom of decisions affecting not only himself but others. Besides, being a husband, sworn and accountable, would doubtless entail inconvenience, if nothing worse, because he had work to do which admitted no other right to his time or energy, and it did not ask for anybody's approval or affection. He vacillated. He said, "The easiest thing in the world is to take a wife, and the most difficult is to get rid of her." But Annette was implacably tenacious in pursuit of matrimony, and grievously incapable of dreaming that it would wed her not only to the man but absolutely to his destiny. No wonder Alberto vacillated. This led to crisis. He resolved it, ultimately, with the sanction of creativity and genius, by saying yes. He had always said yes to life. "Yes" was the answer of the artist, the response of a man dedicated to doing, proof of his devotion to the positive. By agreeing to marry, he agreed to give a fuller measure of his humanity, and his willingness reflects an appreciation of the contribution Annette had already made to that measure. He had experienced a rebirth, had generated new life in his work, so it seems not unnatural that in his personal life he was ready to commit himself to a state which he had heretofore resolutely avoided. He would insist that marriage was not for an instant to be construed as an alteration in any way of his former habits of pleasure and privacy. The very insistence, however, emphasizes the certainty that, on

the contrary, it would alter everything, and Alberto

appears clearly to have been guided by a need to proclaim that he was taking a step directed more toward destiny than matrimony, setting foot on terrain where neither wisdom nor caution could safeguard him. He had been at fault in permitting Annette to join him in Paris. He compounded the fault by consenting three years later to marry her. But the fault—like the awareness of his commitment—was entirely his, and he never attempted to shift or shirk it. He willingly met the cost, which proved to be quite as great as the value added to his art.

Destiny proceeds at its own pace, step after fateful step toward the finality from which it is born. The first few marital years, albeit not made of bliss, were by bohemian standards happy enough. After all, the wildest dreams of Annette Arm as a young woman had come true, for she had made herself the wife of a great and celebrated artist, immortalized by him as a model for the masterpieces enshrined in the world's museums. Now that she was Madame Alberto Giacometti, however, her dreams grew gradually wilder. She wanted to become a mother. No matter that she had been aware from the beginning that her husband was physically incapable of becoming a father. Wifely self-regard had gone to her head, where it found little common sense to argue with the facts of biology. Alberto himself had long since come to a comfortable accommodation with nature. Besides, he did not like, or want, children. And Annette, being quite young enough and silly enough, was herself rather like a daughter. Moreover, as a matter of fact he had provided her with plentiful offspring: works of art in her image.

The transformation from perishable clay into immortal bronze had operated as a symbolic affirmation that the creative passion was potent, achieving a vital intensity that lifted the artist's physical act into a supernatural firmament. That Annette possessed no vision prolific enough to glimpse such a miracle of gestation was not her husband's failing. Her frustration, however, so fed upon itself that its intransigent growth was to nourish the eventual development of a kind of scourge in the marital realm.

People began to see that a previous semblance of contentment no longer portrayed the truth of intimate relations between husband and wife. She now started giving vent, sometimes even in public, to hysterical outbursts of rage and resentment. Her reasons seemed not altogether unreasonable, moreover, especially and maddeningly to her. A recurrent and principal one was material. Slowly and inexorably Alberto was growing rich. Dealers and their agents brought packets of banknotes to the ramshackle studio. Alberto hid them beneath piles of rags, in cupboards, under his bed. Leonardo da Vinci had said, "As for property and material wealth, these you should always hold in fear." Alberto absolutely did. He refused to be compromised by the triviality of ownership or possessions, and felt constrained to live by an ascetic scruple so pure as to appear almost saintly. His preference for privation was a resolve to enjoy life's grandest luxury: spiritual freedom. To Annette, this quest for affirmation looked like self-indulgence, the resolve like pride. They were looking, of course, at different objectives from different points of view. What Annette wanted was a household, the kind of lodging that might comfortably become a home, which could never have been said of 46, rue Hippolyte-Maindron, with its coal stoves, cold water, exterior toilet, and absence even of a telephone. Alberto would heed none of this. He evidently felt that it should suit his wife to live as he did. Annette didn't see it that way at all. Having made the best of things when the going was poor, why should she not expect to do the same when it grew rich? She pleaded and shrieked. He was adamant.

Then the climate of ambivalence and conflict was altered for better or worse by the sudden arrival in Alberto's studio of a philosopher from the other side of the world. Isaku Yanaihara, Japanese, aged thirty-eight, tall, aquiline, and without glasses or camera, had come to Paris from Tokyo for two years of study at the Sorbonne. Already acquainted with Sartre and Simone de Beauvoir, Yanaihara requested an interview with Giacometti in order to obtain more information about his work. Alberto never refused such appeals. The two men found each other interesting. A friendship ensued. The artist proposed to paint the philosopher's portrait. Yanaihara agreed to pose, little imagining to what commitment of emotional energy and physical perseverance he was agreeing. The intimacy between the two men grew intense, began to have the aspect of a passionate attachment, and spilled over from the ascetic studio to the adjoining bedroom. Annette was drawn into it. Amused and intrigued by the exotic Yanaihara, with whom she found herself sometimes left alone when Alberto had appointments with dealers, critics, or other friends, she responded to his polite and persuasive attention with an exhilaration and refreshment presently akin to rapture. The philosopher reciprocated with exquisite ingenuity, and the two became lovers forthwith, openly and optimistically. Alberto observed this precipitation of sentiments with equanimity, not to say with satisfaction. After all, he had always had a private nocturnal life of his own, fiercely guarded, and he greeted with relief the tranquil abatement of his wife's hysterical outbursts. He continued laboriously to paint portraits of the philosopher, each one a challenge to renew the infinitely changeable inferences of vision. This determination to prove that seeing can be believing became concentrated entirely on likenesses of Yanaihara; therefore, when the philosopher had to return temporarily to responsibilities in Japan, which included care of a wife and two daughters, the artist paid for his prompt return to the studio, as well as to the adjacent bedroom, where Annette waited patiently for the resumption of her newfound career as a woman of high passion. These arrangements continued more or less congenially on and off for several years, during which time all seemed to be for the better thanks to them. Such, unhappily, was far from the case, because an indispensable participant in the entire creative endeavor, Alberto's brother Diego, ever present at the artist's side from the very beginning as model, confidant, and collaborator, looked upon the present state of affairs and saw what any fool could easily have seen: that the ground of the Giacometti ménage had decisively shifted beneath everybody's feet. Neither a prude nor a prig, Diego's view of affairs of the senses was a Latin one, and his sister-in-law's behavior seemed scandalous because she was a married woman, because the business was public knowledge, and because, above all, she had extracted matrimony from his brother. As for Alberto's involvement in the matter, this did not seem to Diego anything of which he need take account, since Alberto was a man and an artist. But he did not keep his disapproval to himself. He ceased speaking to Annette unless absolutely necessary, and then but with curt hostility, while to others he openly called her a whore. Alberto, to whom Diego's presence and devotion had from childhood been indispensable, was naturally dismayed, but he didn't know how to resolve the dilemma, trapped as he was in an innocent web of perversity woven by unforeseeable factors that extended far, far down into the deepest extremities of his forgotten infancy. Yanaihara's portraits had become essential to a sense of enriching self-discovery in his work, and Annette's girlish delight in the emotional triangle appealed to the innate generosity of his temperament as well as to a frank predilection toward sexual anomalies. At the same time, however, Alberto was too committed to the intricacies of truth not to recognize, as Diego did, that a decisive juncture lay fatefully underfoot.

It came, characteristically, without warning one tender night in October 1959 when Alberto sat in a rather sleazy bar called Chez Adrien which catered to pimps and prostitutes in Montparnasse, where any artist could enjoy anonymity so long as he was gener- | 93 ous with money. He noticed at the bar an attractive girl whom he considered too young to frequent such a place, so he invited her to have a drink at his table. She accepted. Her name was Caroline, she said, though in fact, as it later came out, this was not her true name. The matter, indeed, of how much about Caroline there was to be found in the realm of truth—even with the most diligent scrutiny—will remain forever tantalizing and unanswerable. This quality inevitably intrigued the observant artist. He talked with the girl till Adrien closed, then they strolled down the boulevard in the first light to an open café and kept on talking till the city had gone to work. Caroline was twenty-one years old. Alberto had just turned fifty-eight and every day of those years had made its mark on his appearance, adding to it the severe dignity of a decade of which he was destined never to see the end. The girl, of course, was a prostitute, but she was also a shrewd and candid critic of experience. About art she knew nothing and cared nothing. Like everyone else, however, she was immediately impressed by Alberto's magnetism, brilliance, charm, and generosity of spirit. He responded with the intensest interest to a propensity for mythmaking in her stories about herself, her adventures in the Parisian underworld and disdain for workaday convention. Only gradually did Caroline gather that Alberto was Alberto Giacometti and that this represented a standing of appreciable nobility. When, and exactly to what extent, they became lovers is expectably unclear. Alberto talked almost too willingly

about the elusiveness of sexual satisfaction, whereas

Caroline had a vested interest in testifying to the contrary. Satisfaction of an essential kind was surely had.

When the sexual rapport brought about the added, supreme distinction of the aesthetic, then the implausible relation between the artist, subtle as a doge and cultured as a mandarin, and the uneducated but meditative girl of the streets became an irrefutable union created by the resourceful footfall of destiny. What Caroline may have thought when she first beheld the tumbledown studio of her lover nonpluses the imagination. Seated before him on a rickety wicker chair as the transfigured object of his creative determination, however, she may soon have seen herself in a guise which would alter forever her view of the world and her situation in it. Alberto's fixation upon the portraits to be painted of his inamorata soon replaced those of the Japanese philosopher in the evolution of his progress toward the visual revelation always one step ahead of him. Yanaihara, in any case, had by now departed for the last time from Paris.

To play up to prostitutes in Montparnasse, praising them as goddesses and idols of womanhood, was one thing. To introduce a prostitute into his private life and into the consecrated precincts of his studio itself, making her the obsessive object both of his artistic and personal devotion—this was to visit a plague upon his realm. Both Diego and Annette, irreconcilable as they remained, were in indignant agreement as to the baneful effect of it. The advent of Yanaihara had been bad, Diego thought; of Caroline, he felt, much worse, a step that might, indeed, bring disastrous consequences. "It makes me physically sick," he said, "to see her sitting in the studio. It's an infection. Even the way she holds her head, it's disgusting." Annette shrieked and wept, demanding that her husband cease all relation with the other woman. But the artist heeded only what he saw, not what he heard. He cared only to be enraptured by his model. If she turned out to be a femme fatale, so much the better. Weren't they all? He longed to possess one part of her body that would become solely and inalienably his own, not to be shared with the other men whom he knew to be her clients. He was prepared to pay, determined, in fact, to pay, for only by paying the price could he be sure of possession, and both knew that. The piece of Caroline he desired to own was a part of her right foot, a very specific part: just above the heel, where two hollows are formed by the Achilles tendon. Some mythic supposition about that part being the most vulnerable may have quickened the purchaser's desire with a notion that his ownership might confer immortality. Who knows? The girl, of course, was willing to sell, but neither party was qualified to appraise the value of the merchandise. Alberto probably sensed that it was priceless, and realized that Caroline had best be protected from such a perilous inkling. They finally settled on the sum of 500,000 francs, equivalent at the time to about a thousand dollars, an amount sufficient to stir the imagination, to stir it, indeed, sufficiently to seem to evoke such a plague as had afflicted Thebes and could only be relieved by the revelation of Oedipus's guilt.

After Yanaihara's final departure from Paris, Annette's concept of herself as a personification of romantic passion was shattered, and she blamed the loss not only on her husband but also on his mistress. There were ugly scenes in public places, Annette shouting recriminations while her husband angrily insisted that Caroline had become "essential to me for my work." The wifely tantrums little by little grew so violent that her weary husband started calling her "The Sound and the Fury," and maybe he did not entirely appreciate the nickname's aptness, situating life midway between idiocy and nonentity as a great man's answer to the prospect of death. Annette accepted it almost as her due, referring to herself as "the S. and the F." though surely never guessing to what tragedy of marital catastrophe the quotation referred. So the tumult matured in acrimony, including now not only the presence of Caroline but also a long-rankling resentment against Alberto's way of life: his refusal to improve the austere lodgings, defiant indifference to his own well-being, and fierce disregard for anything that interfered with his work. Her husband's growing fame also infuriated the censorious wife, because it dismissed her person virtually as much as it glorified her image. For years she had been talking about her desire for a decent place to live, though she knew Alberto would never give up the rue Hippolyte-Maindron. Escaping from Caroline's nightly visits and settling herself in greater convenience and comfort were reasons enough for moving. There were others—and one in particular which over fifteen years had become constantly more oppressive: the light burning night after night by the bedside. With uncanny intuition the wife had hit upon a singularity of

her husband's existence which might most have justi-
fied her eagerness to leave his bed. It was a little like
her long-ago hesitation at the prospect of marrying
a cripple. To be sure, she did not understand the
deeper meaning behind her aversion, for she could
have lived with that knowledge far less well than with
the light, although Alberto once in an outburst of
ominous anger had said to her, "I only married you
because you have the same name as my mother." A
terrible thing to say, but even more terrible to *have* to
say, and nearly unbearable to have to recognize as an
adumbration of truth.

So Alberto sensibly acceded to Annette's longing
for the bourgeois setup from which he had long ago
helped her to flee and bought her a comfortable
apartment. Still, she continued to insist that Alberto
abandon his liaison with Caroline. To no avail. She
ranted and stormed, repeatedly threatening to kill herself should he fail to comply with her rightful demands. She never made an attempt, of course. I once
asked Alberto—a propos of nothing concerning him
personally—whether he ever considered suicide. "Every day," he replied. It was his absolute and oracular
prerogative to say that. Truth is life beyond death, beyond evil, beyond pestilence.

As Giacometti approached the age of sixty he had
long since taken to living and working later and later
in the night. He often worked until dawn before going
to bed, exhausted. A routine like that was far from
salutary. The artist suffered from ill-defined ailments
and pains, neuralgia on the left side of his face, and
stabbing discomfort in his stomach. What was easiest

to diagnose was the constant hacking cough of a smoker. He warned himself in writing: **smoke not too much**! But now he was smoking eighty cigarettes a day, Pall Malls, Luckies, Camels, Phillips, no matter, and the pile of discarded packets stood with the symbolic purport of a pyramid in a corner of the studio. Alberto recognized that he was not in the best of health but did not take kindly to comments on the deterioration of his physical appearance. The lines of his face had grown deeper, and his flesh was the color of clay. Glasses now were needed for his bloodshot eyes. Irregular meals had ruined his appetite, and he complained of the recurrent pains in his stomach. He worried about cancer, but when he awoke after too little sleep his only concern was to get on with his work.

"It's not enough to do what I can do," he said, "but I must do what I cannot do. If I could actually make a head as it is, that would mean one can dominate reality. It would be total knowledge. Life would stop. It's curious that I can't make what I see. To do that, one would have to die of it."

Of all the complaints Alberto suffered from, the most persistent was the most general: fatigue. He was always exhausted, never had enough sleep, rest, relaxation, often talked about being wearied to death. His letters, many of them written in bars late at night, spoke repeatedly of exhaustion. He made no attempt to change. By getting along with so little rest, so little comfort, so little food, Alberto severely reduced his dependence on those needs and wants that inhibit visionary relations with reality. Heightened states of awareness do exist, and they are frequently a conse- | 99 quence of self-mortification. The holy man in his grotto does have mystic experiences and rapturous visions, induced in part by undernourishment, discomfort, and solitude. His sole object—like the artist's—is the observance of a private religion in which he is both the faith and the faithful. That is what sets him apart. Similar detachment can come from chronic fatigue, a kind of intoxication, producing an almost ecstatic sense of perception. But like all intoxicants it bears the danger of addiction, and danger itself can become a stimulation. Alberto's fatigue was essential to his strength. There seemed no limit to his need and acceptance of self-punishment. The reward was to see all things in their vastness by fixing his eye with indefatigable determination upon a single one. To a journalist interviewing Alberto about his relation to his work, he said,

> Art interests me very much, but truth interests me infinitely more. The more I work, the more I see things differently. That is, everything gains in grandeur every day, becomes more and more unknown, more and more beautiful. The closer I come, the grander it is, the more remote it is. For me it would be worthwhile to work even if there were no outcome for others, simply for my own vision, my vision of the external world, of people. But to succeed in portraying that, in portraying a head . . . when I see the face, I don't see the nape of the neck, because it is almost impossible to have any notion of depth from that viewpoint, and when I see the nape of the neck, I forget the

face! Sometimes I think I can catch an appearance, then I lose it and so I have to start all over again. That's what makes me hurry onward. I believe I progress every day. Oh, I believe that even if it's barely perceptible. And more and more I believe that I progress not merely day by day but absolutely each hour. That's what makes me run faster and faster, that's why I work more than ever. I am certain to do what I've never done before and what will make obsolete the sculpture I did last night or this very morning. Even if it's nothing at all, for me it is something more than it was and it always will be. It never goes backward, never again will I do what I did last night. So everything becomes a kind of exhilarating frenzy for me. Exactly like the most extraordinary adventure: if I embarked on a ship for unexplored countries and came upon islands and inhabitants more and more unexpected, it would be exactly like what I'm doing now. That adventure is really and truly mine. So, whether there is any outcome or not, what difference can it possibly make? Whether in an exhibition there are things that succeed or fail, to me it's all the same. Since for me, in any case, everything fails, I would find it quite natural that nobody should pay the slightest attention. I ask for nothing but to continue desperately onward.

He did, and while Alberto modestly persevered in his pursuit of a reality beyond his perception of the real, passersby came to recognize that already for half |

a lifetime they had stood in the presence of a great creator, a unique being of legendary dimension and heroic stature.

All the while, nonetheless, Alberto had to come to terms in normal simplicity with his existence as a man not unlike billions of others, though he realized perfectly well that his body was not the realm in which the decisive contest would be settled. He was obliged to contend with it, however, and to make it do. The sturdiest physique on earth could not have resisted forever the kind of punishment inflicted upon it by Alberto. Fits of coughing, increasingly frequent, seemed to stop just short of suffocation. He was vomiting bile. For years he had suffered from stomachaches and lack of appetite. Abdominal pains became acute. He often had the impression when going to sleep that he might never waken. He dreamed of having cancer and thought that if he must have some disease, that was the one he wanted. Being so grave and mysterious, it had an "absolute" character which made it, for him, the most interesting. And at last, impelled by increasing pain, he returned to the familiar doctor's office. This time, prompted by who knows what notion of responsibility, instead of prescribing some makeshift remedy, Fraenkel sent his friend to consult a surgeon. The latter was none other than Dr. Raymond Leibovici, still practicing in the clinic where he had treated the artist's broken foot a quarter of a century before. If a coincidence, it seemed an auspicious one, for the patient had confidence in Leibovici and was prepared to abide by his recommendation. When the surgeon inspected X-rays of Alberto's abdomen and intestinal tract, he saw at once a large malignant tumor of the stomach, the outgrowth of a ten-year-old gastric ulcer, and he was astonished to think how much pain the artist had endured. Immediate surgery was imperative. Knowing that so radical an operation is never without deadly risk, he chose not to tell Giacometti the truth. As he held up the X-rays and described the surgical measure required, he saw that Alberto studied his face with penetrating scrutiny, but the artist asked no questions and accepted without apparent emotion Dr. Leibovici's assertion that an ulcer was the only trouble requiring surgery.

Though unwilling to disclose the truth to his patient, the physician did follow medical protocol in revealing to Dr. Fraenkel the true facts of the matter. He went even further, informing an overbearing medical man from Bregaglia by the name of Serafino Corbetta who, as Alberto grew famous, had appointed himself official doctor to the Giacometti family.

It was not for nothing that Giacometti had for years dreamt of cancer and regarded it as the most interesting and revealing malady afflicting mankind. He had not questioned Leibovici's explanation, but he was too cautious to entrust his fate to a mere acquaintance whose professional forebears, after all, in prehistoric times had been sorcerers and oracles. So he went directly to the avenue Junot and put the question to Fraenkel. Honoring professional discretion, Fraenkel replied that the trouble was an ulcer, nothing more. Alberto was not satisfied. He demanded that Fraenkel swear by the love of his wife and his mother that he | **103** spoke the truth. Fraenkel swore. Then Alberto was satisfied. But it was almost as if he was disappointed, for he went about saying, "If it were cancer, I'd be willing, because that's an experience worth having. But this is a trifle, a nuisance."

Cancer is a complex disease, arising from the interaction of our organs and cells with numerous factors in the environment. Some physicians have proposed that a predisposition to suffer from cancer may be hereditary, thus a fate unwittingly bestowed by parents upon their offspring. Yet individuals often blame themselves for their illness. The idea that such an aggressive, life-threatening disease arises at random runs contrary to a firm belief in cause and effect. Man's mind can weave the most tenuous strands of information into an imagined cause. People seem peculiarly prone to blame themselves for their illnesses. In some religions, disease is viewed as divine punishment for sin, and it is tempting to rationalize the seeming injustice of a malady by interpreting it as a rightful form of retribution. To what motive, then, should one attribute Alberto's persistent dream of being assailed by the most menacing, mysterious malady that afflicts mankind? Should his fierce resolve to get at the truth explain his relation to so pernicious a condition?

The operation performed on the morning of February 6, 1963, was a partial gastrectomy. Giacometti lay on the operating table for three hours, and Dr. Leibovici was aware as he worked that in such cases one patient out of four would die. But Alberto responded very favorably. By evening it was clear that danger had been averted. The very next day he was out of bed for a few minutes. He had brought with him in a wooden box a small figurine, wrapped in damp rags, and while recuperating he occasionally took it out and fingered the clay. Its responsiveness under those circumstances was a demonstration of his right and sovereign relation to the truth.

Fourteen days after the operation he was able to leave the clinic. To convalesce in necessary comfort, however, he settled in a small hotel rather than his studio. He had made up his mind to travel as soon as possible to Stampa, where his mother would look after him and he could draw her portrait. Dr. Leibovici advised that convalescence must be conscientious, knowing that a danger of recurrence always threatens, though he took care not to say so, insisting only that henceforth his patient must lead an existence disciplined by common sense, which meant regular hours, a well-balanced diet, moderate work, avoidance of fatigue and anxiety, and no smoking—a conduct, in short, utterly contrary to all of Alberto's former habits. The artist listened politely, then consulted his old crony, Dr. Fraenkel, who inevitably advised, "Keep on as before," which was all Alberto cared to hear and was anyway what he had determined to do. The advice was hardly consistent with the Hippocratic oath, but it recognized, at least, the need of an artist to be true to a self over which he has, in any case, no control. And by this very token, a further, ineluctable step had been taken toward the fateful denouement determined from the beginning.

After three weeks of boring convalescence at the Hôtel l'Aiglon, Alberto felt able to travel. He decided | 105 to take the more clement southern route homeward with Annette via the night train to Milan, thence by taxi to Lecco, Chiavenna, and Stampa. Since they would be arriving in Chiavenna about lunchtime, he suggested, why not have it with the gregarious Dr. Corbetta, director of the hospital in that frontier town? Exuberant at the prospect of playing host to the famous artist and his wife, Corbetta greeted them with effusion and during lunch exclaimed, "After all our worrying, you don't know how glad I am to see you here!"

"What worrying?" said Alberto. "It was nothing."

"Oh, you will never know how worried we were," Corbetta insisted.

"What about?" asked Alberto.

"Oh, nothing, nothing," mumbled the portly, obtuse doctor. But it was too late.

"What were you worried about?" Alberto demanded. "If you were worried, it was for something that was worth worrying about. If you're so glad to see me again after so much worrying, then the thing you were worried about must have been the possibility that you might *not* see me again. Was that it?"

The fatuous doctor twisted and turned. It was no good. If he had worried for fear he might not see his friend again, no reason but danger of death can have been persuasive. Corbetta still tried to prevaricate, whereupon Alberto exclaimed, "If you don't tell me the truth, I'll leave here now and you'll never see me again."

So it came out. Leibovici had written his provincial
 colleague a letter, describing in full the operation and

its outcome, concluding with the observation that, although the artist might have a normal existence for a few years, danger of recurrence would always remain. Alberto saw the truth that he had dreamed of. It was the truth of retribution and doom, of life's insecurity and frailty, of fate from first to last always imminent.

Leaving Chiavenna and the injudicious doctor, Alberto was both exhilarated and infuriated. But fury was uppermost, directed against a single person: Dr. Theodore Fraenkel. He had frequently failed as a doctor, but Alberto had never held that against him, had, indeed, seemed almost glad to take for granted the failing of the medical man but by the same token had assumed that the friend would prove infallible. It was from the friend that he had asked for an oath of truth. Alberto had believed it, and one of the great moments of his life had been belittled by a lie. It was unforgivable, and he would never forgive it.

Arriving in Stampa, Alberto had to control himself for fear of alarming his mother, the one person whose wont to worry over him he cherished. He kept the truth to himself. She was overjoyed to find him lively and well. He was almost too lively. Hardly had the time of leisurely homecoming elapsed before Alberto started making lengthy telephone calls abroad. He had to be cautious in his choice of words, because his mother was listening. But he couldn't wait to let others know that he knew what they knew. This was not from a desire to show the stoutness of his spirit. What he wanted was to put himself back into a rightful relation with the truth. If danger existed, it would not diminish his life but enhance it, making every instant valuable and memorable. That was his exhilaration. It would grow and have a life of its own in his work.

For the moment, however, there was Dr. Fraenkel to be dealt with. Fearful of his own anger, Alberto waited twenty-four hours before telephoning. When accused, the doctor stuttered and tergiversated. To no avail; Giacometti's condemnation was total. Betrayal of trust he could not, and never would, forgive. To one who lives for truth, the wanton lie of a trusted friend is almost equivalent to that friend's death. The Theodore Fraenkel whose company Giacometti had enjoyed, whose own need for sympathy and understanding he had befriended for thirty years, had ceased to exist. Worse, he seemed now never to have existed in the first place. The two men were not reconciled, and it appeared to Fraenkel's friends that the loss of Giacometti's friendship took from his life some vital zest. Less than a year later, in any case, he lay dead of a cerebral hemorrhage. Unforgiving to the end, Alberto, when he heard the news, said, "I'm glad he died before I did."

As to his own zest for life, Alberto was in no doubt. Knowing that death had come near, he enjoyed each day of work with a new excitement. Having survived danger, he could be indifferent to danger and live with the exultation of throwing all caution to the winds.

"Maybe I'll be dead in a month," he said. "I have an even chance of pulling through. I'd be glad if I lived for three more years. One year, anyway. And yet

if somebody told me I've got two months, that would

interest me: to live for two months with the knowledge that one's going to die is surely worth twenty years of unawareness."

The end, to be sure, was not yet. But it was nearing. Alberto could sense it, and in his passion to confront the truth he was prepared to make it all his own, to allow it, indeed, to make of him—and his work—whatever it had to. Neither materially nor mythically, of course, could it ever come so long as his mother lived, so long as she never knew the total truth about her firstborn son. How much she knew would forever remain conjecture, but at age ninety-two she had lived a shrewdly inquisitive and resolutely discerning lifetime. She had scrutinized with unflinching perseverance Alberto's work from first to last, and in it, needless to say, his lifetime lay for the intrepid eye as an open book. What knowledge she saw she finally embraced in her fortitude, no less aware than her son that death strikes without surcease, every day and everywhere, ferocious, fatal, blind. Any fear she may have felt would have been for him.

Meanwhile, in Paris, another failure of faith and betrayal of truth in its veriest existential sense had taken place. Nor, alas, was the traitor a weak-willed and incompetent doctor but rather a man famed for his commitment to high principle, a philosopher bound to ideals of probity foreign as the Falkland Islands to a man like Theodore Fraenkel. An intimate friend of Alberto for twenty-five years, author of serious studies of his sculpture and painting, Jean-Paul Sartre had just published an autobiography titled *Les Mots* (The Words). More real to him than whatever they denoted, words, he wrote, were "the quintessence of things," yet his work was directed to the heart as well as to the intellect, while meaning to explore and evaluate the significance of language in human experience. Contemplating the circumstances of his past, Sartre demonstrated his conviction that everything in an individual's existence has a meaning, that nothing in life is truly accidental, and that what may appear to be a mere happening is in reality an act.

Hailed at once as a masterpiece, *Les Mots* was an immediate international success. Built into its glory, however, may be an inherent flaw, inasmuch as the written word has an ambiguous relation to action: it implies a remove from direct experience and effective responsibility, insinuating that an author's passion for putting together words arises from the need to erect a barrier between his vulnerable self and a world indifferent, hence hostile, to the resources of his vocabulary. Himself quite well-versed in philosophy and literature, even including detective stories—though everyone wondered where he found time to read—Alberto must have been impressed by his old friend's analysis of the way in which art takes hold of an artist's life and molds it to suit the needs which art itself creates. This, indeed, was the truth of his own adventure from its fateful outset, a truth, moreover, of which the cumulative and forceful purport was even then moving toward its climactic effect. So it was the sculptor's rude shock suddenly to discover that the writer had summoned *him*, Giacometti, to become an incredible constituent of the verbal structure. This

is what he read:

More than twenty years ago, one evening while crossing the Place d'Italie, Giacometti was run down by a car. Wounded, his leg wrenched, fallen into a lucid swoon, he at first felt a kind of joy: "At last something is happening to me." I know his radicalism: he expected the worst; this life he loved so well that he would not have wanted any other was suddenly overturned, shattered perhaps, by the stupid violence of chance: "Consequently," he said to himself, "I was not made to be a sculptor, nor even to survive; I was not made for anything at all."

Alberto was appalled. The writer's words struck him as unwarranted and unspeakable, struck him as a personal wound, and struck him precisely in the part of himself and of his whole life that he would least have liked to see made publicly false. For a quarter of a century he had repeatedly spoken of the "accident." Alberto's friends knew the details by heart, making it common knowledge that the incident had taken place in the Place des Pyramides, not on the far side of the city in the Place d'Italie, and nobody who was even casually acquainted with the artist could for an instant have supposed that his reaction might have led him to say to himself: "I was not made to be a sculptor, nor even to survive; I was not made for anything at all." In reality, his reaction had in the profoundest reaches of his being been exactly the reverse. It had generated crucial convulsions of his personal and creative life. Sartre's erroneous presumption seemed an outrage to him, a failure of good faith | 111 made all the more outrageous because the prophet of existentialist responsibility had elevated his creed precisely upon the basis of good faith.

Alberto had not needed Sartre to fashion the facts of his lifetime. Life is meaning, not fact, and Alberto knew better than most people that truth creates circumstance. And now, more than ever, now that the search verged upon its purpose, truth was what Alberto most ardently sought. He had no choice but to end the friendship. "It's as if he'd never known me," he exclaimed. "What's the good of knowing someone for twenty-five years if he hasn't understood the first thing about you?" The first thing, indeed, in this case was the very first, the primal thing, which, as a beginning, had not been plainly manifest. The two men were never reconciled. But perhaps, after all, when it came time to look upon the ultimate denouement, the philosopher's fallible manipulating of the truth was in its own way accurate, because it compelled Alberto to weigh human destiny in terms ever more unsparing and yet compassionate according to the truth hidden beneath his own experience and implicit in the self-indulgent fallacy of Sartre. The philosopher declined to acknowledge his responsibility for the estrangement, blaming it entirely on Giacometti.

The regal matriarch of the alpine valley had finally started to weaken. A living link with a past nearer to antiquity than to the present day, she had seemed to guarantee the duration of things that only she remembered. But then her strength began to fail. The family gathered round her in Stampa in the house where she had raised her children. There were moments of vagueness when everyone expected her to expire. But she didn't. Her stamina, like her life, had been made of stouter stuff than the present provided. The three sons waited in the living room, where they had played as children. Alberto spent his time drawing. Then an intestinal grippe set in, at the age of ninety-three fatal. The end came at six o'clock in the evening of January 25, 1964. When it was over, Alberto went alone to his studio, which had formerly been his father's. This studio had all his life been his sanctuary and hiding place. So long as his mother lived, he had never been completely alone there. He could not condone, could not accept, could not understand her loss. Certainly it never occurred to him that his relation to her—and her relation, above all, to his work, in which she had from the first been the vital inspiration—might in any way, however symbolically, be responsible for her death. And yet he called out to her, and the voice in which he called to her was her own voice. He was a prodigiously gifted mimic, able to imitate the most exotic accents. In his mother's voice he called to himself, "Alberto, come eat! Alberto, come eat!" He cried out as Annetta had so often summoned him to the dining room table. "Alberto, come eat!"

Hearing his calls, Annette, his wife, went to the studio and listened but did not intrude. She hurried back and told the others, fearing that her husband, unhinged by his mother's death, was going insane. She need not have worried. Alberto had never been saner.

By calling to himself in his mother's voice to come and eat he was only summoning reality to give him the nourishment which Annetta had provided from the day of his birth. Certainly neither of them had an inkling of the mythological significance, for both of them, of the old lady's death. When the son called out to his mother in his mother's voice, bidding himself to receive from her as he had for sixty-two years the vital sustenance of life, as, indeed, he had received life itself, knowing all the while that she would never do so again, he may somehow have felt that her death was her own doing, thus an acknowledgment of her willingness to abandon him forever, deliberately leaving him alone, as if in retribution for some misdeed of which he had no inkling. As Annetta was borne in the depths of winter to the grave where Giovanni had lain waiting for thirty years beneath the stone designed by her favorite son, was it likely that Alberto failed to remember his seemingly inexplicable behavior at the time of his father's death or his strange inability to be present at the final ceremony in honor of the dead artist? For a man of Alberto's intellect and intuition it seems plausible to suggest that the two deaths should ultimately merge in symbolic inference. His vision itself would appear to have been affected by it, because seeing was for him, after all, equivalent to being. But the mythic denouement would still grant him time, at least, for his last and greatest masterpieces.

Just as his style, his aesthetic purpose and manner of revealing what he endeavored to see, had been vitally altered after Giovanni's death, so it showed a decisive difference when Annetta, too, was gone. Heretofore his tall, thin female figures had conveyed the feeling of primordial votive images, goddesses to be venerated from a distance, unapproachable in their hieratic remoteness. The occasional portraits of family and friends such as Yanaihara or Jean Genet had demonstrated his command of a human likeness. Portraiture per se, with its implied concern for the individuality of the model and care for a convincing physical and psychological likeness, had never been the raison d'être of his creative quest. Portraiture as a genre, moreover, had been in decline for more than half a century. But it was precisely by the making of portraits that Giacometti set out upon the climactic course of his creative adventure. His models were Caroline, Annette, Diego, a friend or two, and, most especially, an acquaintance from earlier years, an alcoholic drifter and personable hanger-on named Elie Lotar. The life that Alberto aspired to impart to them dwelt in their eyes, their gaze, the visual sensation experienced by the concentration of eyes fixed with unflinching intensity upon each other. In this endeavor Giacometti succeeded with such inventive and symbolic vitality that the relation between artist and model often overwhelms the viewer with a power virtually unique in the history of European portraiture.

"The Sound and the Fury" had not abated but only, if possible, grown worse since the death of the majestic mother. The principal cause of Annette's fury, the continued presence of Caroline as Alberto's principal model, was not the only cause of tumultuous reproach. In its acrimony it came to include also the | 115 long-rankling resentment against Alberto's way of life: his refusal to improve the austere lodgings, his defiant indifference to his own well-being, and his fierce disregard for anything that interfered with his work. She stormed and scolded, she said that it was overweening pride. That was true, but so it is, of course, for the hero of every great adventure, and Alberto acknowledged it. He at last acknowledged, indeed, that his wife had legitimate cause for blame. He had led her on. Though he should have known better, he had led her specifically into his studio, where she had surrendered entirely to his demands, albeit transfigured by them. But that had never been truly what she wanted. At heart she had wanted to be cherished as a wife and desired as a woman. It was an unrealistic expectation, but she had not possessed the intellectual wherewithal to assess reality even as it determined the itinerary of her life, much less that of a genius. Alberto recognized this. He was neither a blackguard nor a fool, and he accepted the fault. He welcomed it in the end. Now the truth lay revealed before him in its extremity. He could not blind himself to what he had done. Annette had been used by him, by his work, by his ambition. Even more ruthless than his lucidity was his remorse at having acceded to his own willingness to use her. Forgiveness could not be vouchsafed by knowledge of guilt. He shed real tears, and as he wept he murmured over and over again, "I've destroyed her, I've destroyed her, I've destroyed her." To see tears of guilt and remorse flow from the eyes of a hero was, to say the least, profoundly humbling. But he accepted entire responsibility for everything that had happened. And at the last, which was not yet, his acceptance would be unbearable.

Even as he confronted the guilt implicit in his behavior toward his wife, Alberto began to puzzle over the enigma within the enigma which had always been the origin and inspiration of his relationship with Caroline. Diego from the first had pronounced her a pestilence, her constant presence a plague. Now Alberto started asking himself questions he did not want answered, questions to which he knew the answers but refused until the very end to say even what they meant. Oh, it had been clear enough that she was what she was, an adventuress whose presence came at a cost, a cost in creativity, confidence, and cash which might ultimately on all these counts come higher than the most intrepid prospector could afford. But Alberto still accepted Caroline as she was, because that was the rule of their relationship. If she did, in fact, represent a sort of plague, the duration of its harm would not be protracted now.

Never a man given to foreign travel save between Stampa or Maloja and Paris, Alberto made two important voyages in the summer and autumn of 1965. Both were undertaken to visit large retrospective exhibitions of his lifework, one in London at the Tate Gallery, the second in New York at the Museum of Modern Art. Returning from the longest voyage of his lifetime, Alberto devoted himself almost entirely to his work on the third, final, bust of Lotar. Its finality emanates solely from itself as a terminal statement. This vision is of a man grown ageless in the extremity of old age. Its survival proclaims in supremely Giacomettian terms that as a work of art it is unfinished and represents the unfinishable essence toward which men strive as redemption from the temporal and as atonement for the fateful transgression of their efforts. Capable of this, the artist had nothing left to do but die, bequeathing to the history of mankind his final vision.

Because he felt that the Parisian doctors had deprived him of his right to the truth Alberto went annually for examination to the Cantonal Hospital in Chur, where he believed he could receive an honest diagnosis as to the possible recurrence of cancer. The physician in charge, Dr. M. G. Markoff, was well known in Switzerland and acquainted with the Giacometti family, as his brother had been in school with Bruno. There had been as yet no sign of a recurrence. Having examined Giacometti on two previous visits, Dr. Markoff was shocked in early December 1965 to find his patient exhausted, wasted, breathing with difficulty, presenting clear signs of cardiac weakness and circulatory trouble. He prescribed immediate oxygen, followed by treatment with digitalis and other restorative drugs. Improvement was prompt. From the day of his arrival in the hospital, Giacometti was treated as a person of consequence. Visitors were frequent. Bruno and his wife, Odette, came from Zurich, Diego and Annette from Paris. Even Caroline appeared for a couple of days. But Dr. Markoff did not deem his patient as yet physically fit to be discharged.

A few days before Christmas, Alberto's condition inexplicably took a turn for the worse. The circulatory

trouble became more pronounced, while the heart

muscle functioned with increasing difficulty, causing serious congestion of the pleurae and liver. As he lay in the hospital room, aware that his condition was serious, if not fatal, Alberto cannot have failed to contemplate a future in which the person known as Alberto Giacometti would have ceased to exist. When told by a worried friend that the doctors could not restore his health unless they had his cooperation, he said, "I can no longer give my cooperation."

In the first days of the new year, Dr. Markoff observed that his patient's condition had now grown grave. He was breathing with increased difficulty and the heart muscle had weakened further. It was the result of a lifetime of chronic bronchitis, all those decades of drastic coughing, eighty cigarettes a day, chronic fatigue, and lifelong anxiety. It was the result, in short, of implacable self-punishment. His guilt had found him out at last, and found him ready. "I've certainly done everything I could in order to end up where I am now," he observed. And so he had. From the beginning in the cave. From the death in the Italian mountains. From the "accident" in the Place des Pyramides. From first to last he had labored to give life to his vision. This had been his oracular truth and he did not falter from its ultimate fulfillment. One more aspect of mythic determinism may now seem to have been realized.

To the nurses, he said, "I'm going mad, I don't know myself anymore. I no longer have any desire to work."

His whole life had been based on the equivalence of seeing to being. He knew who he was by seeing | 119 what he did. The person he had always before any other desired to see and to depict had been his mother. Late in the afternoon of Monday, the tenth of January, 1966, while alone with Markoff in his room, Alberto murmured to the doctor, "Soon again I'll see my mother." Just two years previously, Annetta had lain dying in Stampa. Now his own death was imminent. To see his mother again would be the confirmation and consummation of all he had done, all he had been. Throughout his life, his vision of her had repeatedly been the supreme affirmation of reality. To be united with her in the sight of eternity was his dying wish.

The next evening he lay dead, his eyes sightless precisely because, as he had said, he had certainly done everything he could in order to come to that end, blinded by a fate which had been settled before his birth.

AFTERWORD

Some commentators on mythology have viewed Oedipus in his indomitable pursuit of the truth as a personification of light, and his self-blinding as the disappearance of the sun at the end of the day, thus the origin of darkness. Alberto, had he known of such an interpretation, might well have found it persuasive, as he foresaw no future for the sort of creative adventure which had been his. So tragic a view he knew how to endure. Whether his contemporaries possessed comparable strength is debatable. Speaking of abstract art not long before his death, he noted:

It creates a self-contained object, as self-contained and as finished as a machine, without reference to anything beyond itself. Now the question arises of how to define this new kind of creation. One wonders what might become of abstract sculpture and abstract painting. How would a Brancusi statue look if it were chipped and broken, or a Mondrian painting if it were torn or turned dark with age? One wonders whether they belong to the same world as Chaldean sculptures, as

Rembrandt and Rodin, or whether they form a world apart, closer to that of machines. I would go further and ask to what extent they may still be defined as sculpture, as painting. How much have they lost of the meaning in these words? Painting as we know it? I think it has no future in our civilization. Neither does sculpture. What we might call "bad painting"—that has a future . . . there will always be people who would like to have a picturesque landscape, or a nude, or a bouquet of flowers hanging on the wall . . . but what we call great painting is finished.

This was Alberto's melancholy farewell to the creative fatality to which he had given his life. He did well to die when he did.

By way of conclusion, it seems proper to emphasize, as I did at the outset, that the purpose of this lengthy and speculative essay has never been to suggest that the life of Giovanni Alberto Giacometti was a replica, so to speak, or even a predetermined representation of the mythological existence of Oedipus, King of Thebes, hero of the drama by Sophocles, a figure whose legend fascinated people in antiquity and has not failed to do so since. There are, however, aspects of Alberto's life from the beginning which repeatedly—one may again say insistently—evoke the Oedipus myth and complex. I have recorded them chronologically and need not recapitulate now. It is up to the reader, should anyone be interested, to try to fathom the interest. Great art, after all, creates what is most profoundly interesting and important about man's brief sojourn in his lonely world. As for myself, I believe that Alberto Giacometti's destiny, his labor in search of truth, and his self-sacrifice for it are admirably complex, as well as consistently puzzling, and in the most durable sense of the term: mythic.

INDEX

DATE DUE

			Printed in USA

HIGHSMITH #45230